# THE BURDEN OF HOPE

# The Burden of Hope

*Finding Color in a Black & White World*

## by David Kranz

ISBN: 978-0-578-87151-6

Cover design and typesetting by Stewart A. Williams
Cover photograph Matthew Smith on Unsplash

First edition printing 2021

*Dedicated to all of those who have identified as "That Kid". Even on your hardest days, find the light in yourself to guide you through the darkest times.*

"May the God of hope fill you with all joy and peace in believing, so that by the power of the Holy Spirit you may abound in hope."
—ROMANS 15:13 ESV

# From David

Jessica- Thank you for being with me through the deepest and darkest journeys in my life. Your support and strength has been so dearly treasured.

My father-Thank you for every lesson you have ever taught me. For every step you took for me and with me. You have been the most impactive man in my life and greatest mentor. Though I took the steps to change our path of our family name and create something new, you helped guide me down the paths. We have been to hell and back with one another and you have embedded the meaning of how to be a caring father to my own children. You are a great man and I love you dearly. Thank you for all of your support in everything I have done.

Laura Feffer- Thank you for always being there to offer guidance and support. You as well as the rest of the Allegan Alternative High School staff have played such a pertinent role in my development as a person. I have always held you all so very close to my heart. The love and care you devoted to your students has always been remarkable. The genuine support you all have given to each of the student's well-being has certainly left a permanent mark on the world for the better. You were one of the first people to give support and push my writing to inspire me to do much of what I have done today. Thank you all so much.

Levi Wahlers-You have been a friend for many years and even more so a brother. You journeyed with me through many of the events discussed throughout this book and guided me through some of the darkest paths I have ever taken. Your companionship as a brother and support of writing this book has meant so much to me.

Michael Bush-Thank you and the entire fire department for your support. As my "family" in the fire service, the support you all have given in chasing my dreams means so much to me. I know there are times many of you had probably been tired of hearing about "my book", but you did not let me quit. Thank you.

## Special contributions:

Liz Cary, Mandie Weber, Shawn Bennett, Sherry Marden, Jason Smith, and Lon Schafer-Thank you all for taking time to preview this book for me. It has been a privilege to be able to share my story with you before the rest of the world. Your contributions and feedback have provided insight as well as allowed me to reflect honest feedback. Thank you very much.

# Contents

# Introduction

A father and son stood silently beside one another under the moonlit sky. They drifted peacefully as the waves calmly brushed against the wooden boat. The wind gently caressed their hair as the sweet aroma of the ocean offered peace amid the open water. As the clouds passed by gently cloaking the evening stars all seemed well. The father and the son enjoyed the tranquility together as they began their adventure. Yet, as the two drifted, subtle taps could be heard in the distance. The taps became eerily closer turning from taps to splashes and splashes to crashes. As it rapidly approached the boat, hastily reaching closer and closer, the father pulled his son close as the once calm water erupted to a violent rage atop the ocean's surface. The two looked up and a red aura filled the skies while the drifting clouds looked down in contempt. The boy once again looked to the sky to see what tyranny threatened their sanctuary. The world as they knew it began crashing down in a fiery fury. As hellfire rained down around them, the father looked to his son with a calming gaze and softly spoke to him,

"It will be okay."

Embracing his son as the flames faded away, darkness once again filled the sky. Only then did I awake.

This is the dream I once had. For as long as I could re-member it was my father and me against the world. Soon I would realize that the world would intend to fall apart around me, crashing down at every opportunity to tear me apart and swallow me whole. This dream would strike me at the heart, reminding and encompassing every trial I had ever encountered. This though would be the moment I could realize that everything would be okay. Combin-ing the trials of my life I would soon learn that only then could I solidify success and resilience. However, success and resilience could only be obtained through the forging of gruesome trials.

For many years I had sheltered my experiences and trials, labeling them as normal, believing I was nothing unique. I spent much time reflecting on my life wonder-ing, "What makes David so unique? Everyone has strug-gles and hardships, what makes me so special?" Yet, as I began opening up to people close to me about my story, I kept hearing the same responses. The interest could be heard in their voice. Questions surged grasping for more detail. Some described what they heard as unbelievable or terrible. Once I began sharing these stories and elab-orating on experiences through counseling, my therapist expressed that though everyone struggles; based on stud-ies of resilience I was destined for failure from the start. Though, somehow despite the studies and statistics, I de-feated all of the trials and overcame some of the most de-bilitating experiences few could imagine.

I was not able to grasp this for the longest time. How could I ever see outside of my lens when the scope was so small? So isolated. Kidnapping, betrayal, substance abuse, alcoholism, mental illness, physical abuse, incarceration, and ultimately the loss of the unity of nearly all I shared blood with. The list became compounding of the world I grew to know. These were the chains that confined reality to a distorted perception of what normal really was.

Many years have since passed since I've closed those doors, however, reflection has been a never-ending constant. I would not change any of it for the world. Without these experiences, I would not be who I am today. Through all of the shattered pieces and distorted concepts I've endured; they have given me a gift that can only be forged in the most abysmal hell. That gift is molded through tremendous trials, and that gift is resilience.

For the first time, I am able, confident, and ready to share this journey with my readers. To walk side by side with me to peer into another dimension. Or rather, for some, to understand that perhaps I do know what you as the reader are experiencing in your own life? Even if I can only impact one, to help someone else realize they are not alone; and maybe it is not my journey they see as they read, but instead a reflection of your journey. Regardless, it is my goal and desire that whatever you as the reader are experiencing you may find solace as you read. You may find hope, strength, and comfort in knowing that though not all nightmares are when we are sleeping; there is a way out. A better life awaiting all of us as long as we are willing to reach for it.

My name is David Kranz and this is my story.

# The Glass Casket

It was 1983 in Grand Rapids, Michigan. My father John, a sixteen-year-old boy at the time, had dedicated his life to the art of magic. Performing illusions and card tricks, it took years of practice to take hold of the few short minutes of awes from the crowds.

Down the busy road of 28th street at the once busy Eastbrook Mall lay a mystical magic shop-called Merlin's Magic. John volunteered his time at the magic shop working with his mentor and ultimately a man who would become his lifelong best friend and father figure, Paul Scott. Having never known his father, John and Paul bonded through the shared passion for magic and the arts.

One day while John was working the counter, pulling costumes from boxes and placing them up on the old wooden shelves. Glass cabinets lined the dimmed room filled with mysticism and gadgets, gag gifts, and party poppers. A middle-aged couple walked through the door as the bell rang, alarming their presence to John.

"Good afternoon!" John remarked as he greeted them. "Is there anything we can help you find today?"

Patty and Bill Pennington glanced through the odd capacity room of costumes and magical props. They turned to acknowledge the young boy who was greeting them.

"Hello" They exclaimed.

As they browsed the items filling the cabinets, Patty turned to John,

"How old are you?" She inquired.

John, slightly caught off guard, turned and responded.

"Sixteen ma'am", he replied.

"You know, we have a beautiful daughter that I am sure you would just love to meet! She is very intrigued by all of this show business stuff. Maybe she could help you in your magic show!". Patty insisted, bragging her daughter up to the young store clerk.

"I would be pleased to meet her." He responded politely, nodding in agreement.

Though he found the request rather odd, he continued stocking items back into the shelf. It wasn't everyday someone tried to introduce their daughters to him.

"Unfortunately I have a lot of work to do today, perhaps another time?"

After browsing around the shop the two agreed to try and set up a day to meet their daughter. The following Saturday Patty and Bill drove their daughter from Ionia to Grand Rapids to introduce their fourteen-year-old daughter to the young magician. While waiting in anticipation, John had been lounging at the magic shop. While he tinkered with a deck of cards, the glass door emitted a loud and obnoxious "ding" as the bell rang.

A slender, long dark-brown haired woman passed through the doorway. As her beautiful brown eyes reflected off of the few dim lights of the shop; the two locked eyes. As if stuck in time, the two remained startled, frozen in place, two exuberant smiles equally slipped across their shy faces. The rosy red cheeks of the girl began to blush as John approached her.

"Hello," he said, "I'm John" as a cheesy smile emitted across his face.

Lily looked to him in equal regard,

"I'm Lily" she began, "my parents told me about you, and that you may be looking for some help with your magic shows?"

John, still starstruck by the beautiful woman that emerged, tried to fumble the proper combination of words from his mouth,

"I--err--well, I will be performing in November for the Amway" He muttered, scratching his head as it leaned to one side, subtly trying not to break eye contact with her.

"Perhaps we could try and set up a day to do a tryout?"

"That sounds fun!" She giggled.

The two continued to speak as they began the planning of their newfound relationship. Hitting it off almost instantly the two found themselves embarking on a magical journey, professionally, and emotionally. The two remained in contact as they continued their rehearsals for their first upcoming gig. Lily, having been a phenomenal dancer already, took well to the proficiency of stage presence. While she stunned John with her comfortability and compatibility as an assistant; he couldn't be happier and more attracted than he was as he watched her float across the stage in a dazzling performance.

Finding themselves both in Ionia one evening, John had been invited to perform with another mentor of his, Neil Foster. Neil was a nationally recognized performer that John had admired for his crafty sleight of hand. After the show, John and Lily had been invited to a supper party at the local Legion Hall where Patty could not help but brag that her daughter would be performing with her new boyfriend. Her daughter would be a magician's assistant! The night eventually came to an end. But not before Patty filled John's ear with;

"You know, Bill and I are quite the performers ourselves." She began, "Maybe our band could join you and our daughter on stage at the upcoming event?" She pryingly requested.

"I can see what I can do" John replied.

Slightly annoyed at the request, John obliged. Having spent some time rehearsing with Lily and falling in love with her; the last thing he wanted to do was anything off-putting to the Pennington's.

November eventually approached and the two new love birds awaited backstage to be the second act of the evening at the Amway Grand. John arrived wearing a tuxedo, and Lily in a dress with glistening, sparkly, reflective dots all over her skirt. The two looked astounding. Patty and Bill took the stage with their band as they prepared to be the first show of the evening, or so they thought. The crowd sat and looked to the stage as Patty and the band finished connecting their wires and guitars to the many electrical appliances. With her guitar in hand, the lights began to dim while the spotlights shined down focusing on the band.

Patty reached one hand to the microphone, closed her eyes, and prepared to sing. With the other hand, she reached down as she slid her hand up to grip the neck of the guitar. All of a sudden the room froze. The moment

Pattys fingers touched the strings of the guitar with one hand and the other grasped the microphone, she suddenly locked up, her jaw clenched, and a loud electrical pop was heard echoing across the stage.

Somehow, while connecting their equipment, someone had accidentally reversed the polarity of the microphone. Completing the circuit with a much disturbing reaction, Patty was now being electrocuted, on stage for all to see. Bill, having put all of his infinite wisdom to use, unsure of what to do as his wife Patty is being shocked on stage, draws back. With one quick fell swoop his fist connected with Pattys' face. In front of the audience, his band, and his poor wife, he cold cocked her right across the jaw with a very connective right hook. Once he broke the contact of the electrical current Patty fell to the ground in a daze. Quickly the curtains fell and the lights dimmed. The crowd was left in utter dismay while they tried to grasp what had just happened. Though Patty would recover fully, she was in no condition to continue the performance.

The stage manager quickly rushed to John and Lily who both were unaware of the events that had just transpired,

"You two, I need you to the stage now! You're on!". He said excitedly.

John and Lily grabbed their props, took a deep breath, and entered the now-empty stage to perform. The curtains rose as John emerged in his white tuxedo. The lights gave focus to his presence on the stage. The crowd, still recovering from the confusion from the last "act", sat in silence.

Music played as John opened both arms in a show of stunning appeal to the crowd. Lily quickly followed behind him while the lights flickered off her shiny skirt. A box was brought on to the stage as John introduced what most would fear to be the doom of the beloved assistant. The box, which much resembled a square coffin on stilts, such as a table would, was presented to the audience. John unlatched two of the latches on either side of the box, separating it into two. Showing that both boxes were empty, he quickly and gently reconnected the two as he directed Lily to climb into the box. He grabbed her hand and scooted a stool to the base of the connected boxes. As their hands interlaced John assisted Lily up the steps as she slowly climbed inside the box and laid down. Her feet pressed through the two cut out holes of one end while her head laid visible to the audience on the other. John secured her to the box and strapped her in place. The audience stared, wondering what events may follow.

As the audience sat silent, two large blades were produced by John from a wooden rack that rested just in front of the curtain. The reflecting light from above shined down on them as he clashed the blades together showing their authenticity of realism. He grabbed the first blade, looked to Lily, then back to the audience before thrusting the first blade right through the torso of his assistant. The crowd gasped in unison, as another lady near the back of the auditorium let out a scream of shock. "Oh my goodness!" She exclaimed.

Moments later he would thrust a second blade through the torso of Lily.

Two blades now penetrated right through John's assistant as she laid in the wooden box. At this time, the audience, which was moments ago gasping in astonishment, sat silent, waiting to see what was to happen next. John spun the box around once again, showing all sides as he approached and un-clicked one side of the box. Circling it like prey he approached the other side and released the last latch. Nothing held the two segments of his assistant's body together now. He parted the two boxes while the audience again let out a brash gasp as the woman was split into two right before their very eyes. From that moment, his audience was hooked. He re-connected the two boxes and re-latched both sides once again. Slowly he pulled out the first blade, quickly followed by second, only then to reveal his assistant. Lily emerged from the box in one piece, fully restored with no marks to be seen. The audience, pleased by this magical event, stood and applauded as it echoed through the banquet hall. John and Lily looked to one another, smiling and pleased, they turned back to the audience hand in hand to take a bow.

After much success from the show, the two grew closer to one another. Not just in trade, but courtship as well. The two became inseparable. From magic conventions to work, from fairs to movies. It grew to become such a comfortable relationship the two soon found themselves together. Nearing his eighteenth birthday, John eventually moved in with Lily and the Pennington's. This lasted for only a short while as the two learned that though they very much desired to be together, the world would forever try to keep them apart. After only a few short weeks in the Pennington household, John learned the real travesty that lay in the wake in the home. Bill was not the caring father and musical man that John had met at the magic shop. Rather, he found that Bill instead was an abusive drunk. As John witnessed the physical abuse in the home he could no longer stand aside and watch. He eventually stood up to Bill until it became so bad that the state finally became involved. Much to John's dismay, Lily was removed from her home and placed in foster care.

John, heartbroken and distraught, was eager to ride in on his white horse and shining armor. He soon found a way to resolve this blasphemy that threatened their relationship. The two would run away together. In March of 1985 in the early morning, John arrived to take her away. Hitchhiking from Ionia, they made their first stop at a friend of John's in Otsego, Michigan. Jim, his friend, owned a local pizza parlor where the two hid for a short while and grabbed some much-needed food. The two continued on the road, hitchhiking from Indiana to Florida, Florida to Texas, Texas to California and California to Las Vegas. Eventually, the couple's journey ended when they found out they could not be married. Even in Las Vegas, they could not marry at their current age; especially without parental consent. Disheartened, they hitched a ride to Utah. That was the closest to home they could get from their free-riding adventure. Eventually, John built up enough courage to call his mother. Furious at the idea of the two of them roaming the country; John's livid mother purchased a Greyhound ticket to return them both to Michigan.

John and Lily laid low for months at his mother's house until May of 1985. Bill had heard a rumor that the two were staying at John's mothers and had recklessly attempted to reclaim Lily. One evening when John and Lily were returning from a walk; Bill had been waiting just a short distance away for them to return. As the two approached the house Bill, unknowingly to them, emerged and chased after the two. Caught off guard, John and Lily ran to the end of the street trying desperately to escape the rabid father. Bill tackled Lily to the ground while John continued on foot at Lily's request. That was until the police department had caught up with, and arrested John only a few short hours later. Bill had called the cops and claimed that John had stolen a gun and taken Lily against her will. Soon, however, they found that not only was it false, but rather, Lily was to be placed back in the foster home due to her abusive and neglectful father. As a result, the two found themselves before a judge. This time, however, they would finally be granted their much-awaited marriage. The judge signed off and agreed that John and Lily could marry. They had done it. They were free from the treacherous grasp on the Pennington household. This was only the beginning of the Kranz family curse. A curse that would mark our names for years to come.

It was a dark and rainy October evening. Less than a year since the two newlyweds began their journey on their own after escaping the grasps of the Pennington household. John had been away at work and was ready to be home with his wife Lily and their nine-month-old son, John Jr. He turned down the residential street with the lights from the street lamps illuminating off of the wet, dark pavement. John pulled into the driveway after a daunting long week of working. He wiped his eyes trying to stay awake from his drive back before reaching across the seat of his green Monte Carlo to gather his jacket. Stepping out of the car John looked to the doorway with the rain trickling down his weary face. His chest began to tighten as his eyes widened; as if he was just sucked into a black hole. All the while, the world around him began to sink. Looking to the doorway his heart began pounding in his chest. Lily stood under the porch light in the open doorway. Screaming and ecstatic, she stood with her arms out in front of her as pale, lifeless, glossy arms, and legs draped down to either side. Less than twenty feet away from John, baby John lay lifeless in her arms.

A piercing scream erupted from Lily's mouth.

"HE'S DEAD! OUR BABY IS DEAD!" she screamed.

Frantically, John threw the jacket to the hood of the car and rapidly dashed to baby John, quickly scooping him into his arms, and rushing inside the home. He laid little John on the ground and began passionately pressing upon the baby's chest, two fingers into the cold, blue, porcelain doll-like chest.

"One, two, three, four, five, six..." he chanted, as emotion overwhelmed him.

"...Thirty"; he gasped, trying to absorb as much air as he could. Quickly he tilted the head, placing his lips around baby John's, giving his oxygen to the child with two heartfelt breaths. Still, John Jr. remained lifeless.

"One, two, three, four"; he continued.

Lily desperately plead in the corner, timidly frozen, and frightened. John and Lily's son, their firstborn, not a week after muttering every father's much desired first words of "dada", was now fighting for his life.

The ambulance arrived after what had felt like a lifetime. The paramedics emerged hastily through the door with their bag of supplies. Side by side they approached my father, they dropped to their knees and began tirelessly continuing resuscitation efforts. Pulling every tool from their bag, every skill rapidly flowing through their minds; and yet it was too late. The world stood still and the heavens wept as the most debilitating words slipped through the trembling lips of the Paramedic.

"I'm so sorry," said the medic, forcefully trying to push the words from their throat.

"We have tried everything we ca--can...".

Not one dry face remained in the room as the time of death was spoken for baby John. My mother let out the most gut-wrenching scream as the debilitating words flooded her ears. Flailing and heart-broken she collapsed to the floor on her knees near her baby boy. Taking in every last bit of the sweet smell of his silky hair. The soft-touch of her baby's skin. The once warm filled body of every mother's truest love, her son.

My father asked the nearly equally emotional medics if they could give anything to his distraught wife Lily.

"Please!" He asked. "Do you have anything to calm her down!"

A sedative was drawn up and administered to her as she began to slowly drift from the reality of losing her firstborn child.

As the medical examiner arrived to remove baby John, John stepped into the other room to call his brother who lived just a short distance away in Grand Rapids.

"Fred," he said. "I need you to come down here. I need help removing the crib and toys from the house before Lily wakes up."

Fred held the phone in his hand, confused about the request, "What are you talking about?" He inquired, puzzled.

"John Jr. is dead. I don't have time to explain. I just need you here now!" John exclaimed.

Trying to grasp the rapid events that had just been disclosed to him; Fred gathered his wallet, keys, and jacket and rushed out the door. Days would pass as the home remained absent of the once cheerful coos of their infant son. Any color or joy that once filled the home was now absorbed with despair.

Some time had passed as the two young lovers tried to adjust to their new life without their son. Day by day emotionally rebuilding and confronting the daily responsibilities that yielded no mercy to the pain and suffering. John continued to work and Lily coped as well as she could. A year passed when Lily broke the news to John that they were expecting another child. Slightly fearful, yet excited at the news, they soon found they were expecting another child; a little girl. In 1987 a beautiful baby girl was born, Isabelle. Isabelle being the second child and the first daughter, both were excited. They were ready to have those dreaded sleepless nights back as the coos of her baby voice echoed through the house at all hours. The soft skin and the sweet, refreshing, and calming touch of another baby. Not forgetting baby John; they had another love to tend to. Another year elapsed as they soon found more news was to come. Another child was to be expected. In 1988 Lily gave birth to yet another baby boy. Baby Nicholas.

Lily screamed in agony. Sweating profusely, she grasped the rails on either side of the hospital bed. Bright lights shined down to the back of the doctors and nurses towards Lily. The lights glimmered off of the stainless steel trays surrounding the bed with various gowns and utensils. As she breathed deeply the doctors and nurses surrounded her attempting to soothe and support her.

"Just one more big push. You're doing great." One nurse said encouragingly.

John stood to the side of the bed attempting to hold Lily's hand to render comfort.

"You're doing great babe. Just breathe." He said.

"AAAAGGGGG," she screamed in pain, ready to give up. Cries could be heard after one last vigilant push from Lily.

Suddenly relief was felt as the doctor spoke the much-anticipated words of

"Here he comes!"

Nearly nine months had elapsed. After the many appointments and check-ups for their baby boy to arrive, the medical technology was not ready to prepare the two for what would come next. While the two prepared for what should have been a joyous moment, something troubling was waiting in the dark to plague the concept of happiness for Lily and John once again. Baby Nicholas was to be born, however, something wasn't right. As birth was given to little Nicholas, to the surprise of the two, as well as the doctor and nurses, the infant no larger than the palm of my father's hand emerged. Startled, and equally loving as much as concerned, they were to find that the torso was disfigured. Portions of what should have been skin covered, instead exposed organs. Gray tinted skin colored the baby boy's blood-covered body. Something was truly wrong. Not long after, much to their despair, another boy was lost to a world that has laid claim to the Kranz family household. As if a side script of the Book of Job; what trials must they further endure? How much more anguish could be presented to them to test their faith? Disheartened and broken they had yet again found themselves burying another baby boy.

# Little Hellion

After so much despondency, my father and mother could not bear any more grief of loss. After the horrendous reality of burying two sons already, the anxiety and fear were overwhelming. This is where my journey began. I was it. I was the last child.

Perhaps this birth was a sign, however, being born on Mother's Day. What more could a mother ask for than her gift of a child? It was 1989 in Grand Rapids, Michigan; Mother's Day. I was born into what I would learn to be an abyss of pain and misery. A curse bestowed on our family to challenge our very essence in the face of adversity. Not without the reward of course.

What more could a child want than to have two parents, a home, and food? I had a beautiful older sister that loved me. We were a happy family, not quite the Partridge, but certainly trying to rebuild from previous events. Shortly after I was born we moved to South Bend, Indiana. This was where a majority of the early years began. My father received a major opportunity to be the primary face of a well-known industry. With his extensive background in magic, and his ability to perform as a clown, what better opportunity than to become Ronald McDonald himself? As a young man with two kids and a wife, the pay was right to allow the young family to assert their independence. We moved into an apartment complex in Mishawaka. It was just outside of South Bend and only a few minutes from the infamous Notre Dame.

From the beginning, I knew I had a unique family. My father being a traveling performer as the pale-faced, red nose, and red-haired clown; and my mother was a magnificent ballroom dancer. It was seldom that my sister and I would have both parents in the same room at the same time, as my father performed seven hundred shows a year traveling as America's favorite burger mascot. On occasion my mother assisted in my father's shows dressing up in the various costumes that would accompany my father on stage; as a talking burger thief, a purple lump of fur, or a jazzy moon man.

When she was not assisting my father, my mother spent most of her evenings dancing in elegant ballrooms. It was fun to go and visit her at work. She helped instruct couples ranging in all ages how to waltz and salsa across fancy surfaced floors. She brought my sister and me with on occasion. We were allowed to venture through the notorious Dan O'Day Dance studio. It was held on the second floor of an old strip mall in Mishawaka. Before all of the guests arrived, we would trample across the glossy wood floors, going from room to room seeking whatever imaginary adventure we could conjure up. The smell of stale beer and spirits filled the air. It was quite repulsive to the senses of a child, but well worth the cost to have free reign of exploration through caves, dungeons, and castles we could imagine running through.

At times after a long night of dancing my mother

rested during the daytime while my father was away. This was every child's dream and every parent's nightmare. My father was on the road performing, and my mother wore down with the responsibility of keeping an eye on two children, eventually hired a babysitter to assist during the day. One day, however, while my mother laid asleep in her bedroom, our babysitter let the dog out. When she opened the sliding glass door from the living room to the outside world, little did she know our dog Scotch would leap at his five minutes of freedom as he dashed out the doorway; escaping the grasps of the babysitter before a tether could be attached to his collar. This was not just an opportunity for Scotch to explore the world, but it also rendered an opportunity for me to explore. With a wide-open door and no accompanied supervision, I was free to roam.

Unbeknown to my mother or babysitter, I had left the apartment and set out on a journey. At three-years-old I set out on an adventure. Walking down the sidewalk, I ventured through the many side streets of the apartment complex. I soon found myself at an intersection. Not knowing that traffic does not revolve around me, step by step I would walk right into the intersection of the busy roadway on Edison Street. As I navigated through the astounded traffic, a large city bus came to a screeching halt." SCREEEEECHHHHHHHHHHH" as the tires locked and the presumably startled passengers jolted forward in an unannounced stop, the driver shifted into park and exited the bus, hurrying around the large vehicle to snatch up the aimless three-year old seemingly wandering to his death had she not been there.

"Where are your parents?!" She asked.

As my mother was awoken by the baby sitter,

"David took off!" The sitter screamed frantically. "I don't know where he went!"

My mother, half-dazed from a deep sleep jumped to her feet to take foot on a search for her missing son. Without a thought to wear shoes or a jacket, she ran out the door.

"David. David." She yelled, hoping to gather a response from her nearby son.

Yet, no response came. Looking to the pond that my sister and I would frequent on our family walks, mother hastened to the shore.

"David!" Looking at the water she yelled again. Growing drastically more worried she began descending into the mucky, catfish-filled brown water.

"David! Where are you?" She shouted. Again, no response.

She called to some maintenance workers who were nearby, soliciting assistance in finding her missing child.

"Have you seen a little boy walking around here?" She asked.

The men denied seeing a child walking through unaccompanied by anyone. As the catfish nibbled at her now cold and wet feet beneath the water; she turned and looked to the roadway.

She noticed a large crowd of people in the roadway and traffic on a typically busy roadway at a complete standstill. Jumping from the water, escaping the awkward gnaws of the catfish, she ran to the street. As she approached the roadway, a large crowd began to part for her as our crying mother entered the circle to find a three-year-old little boy speaking with a kneeling bus driver. As the crowd scowled at her, she scooped me up in her arms.

"Oh my God baby, I was so worried! What were you thinking?" She muttered, frantically trying to catch her breath and slow her heart rate that had been rapidly pounding at her chest.

"I wanted a Slurpee!" I exclaimed.

She nuzzled my head into her shoulders, with her arms wrapped about my small body, holding me close.

Thanking the pedestrians and the driver, she carried me back towards the apartment complex. She herself lowering her head in shame as the scolding looks surrounded her.

Eventually, I found myself in similar circumstances of testing my limits with my mother. Even after this event, the routines would persist. Due to the long nights at the dance studio, and the frequency of my father's absence, I had always found a way to give my mother an exciting story for my father to hear about upon his return. One afternoon while my mother was sleeping I found a lighter resting at the head of her bed. Not knowing the full potential danger of my next steps, but being rather intrigued by the dancing beauty of fire I snatched it up. Walking into the bathroom that was attached to my mother and father's bedroom, I could hear the toilet paper taunting me. It rested just below the light switch near the toilet. "Flick" "flick" "flick" the lighter sparked as the gear rolled against the flint. After several attempts I was able to produce a good enough spark. In the perfect combination of holding down the button while the gear clicked, I produced enough fluid to create the fiery hot combination for a flame. I held the lighter with one hand as I grabbed my first strip of toilet paper allowing the fire to gracefully engulf the first piece.

Astonished, and standing in awe, I dropped it into the toilet as the ash and paper hit the water letting a subtle "Hiss" echo from the porcelain bowl. It was invigorating. Knowing how one piece would react I again replicate my previous steps. "Flick, flick, flick" again, creating a flame. This time, however, instead of removing a strand of toilet paper from the roll attached to the wall; I touch the tip of the flame to the tail of paper from the roll calling my name. It just wanted me to create a little bit bigger of a reaction this time. This time though would prove just how reckless the flames can be. As the flame touched the base of the paper, it ignited and took off like a wick to a fire-work. Flames trailed up the wall scorching the paint and drywall as it went. In frantic desperation, I scooped water into my hand splashing the violent, flaming, toilet paper roll. Once again, "hiss".

My mother, again startled by the commotion created just a few feet away, and the chirping of the smoke alarm, rushed in to see what had happened. Startled and flustered she snatched the lighter from me, spanked my butt, and with a pointing finger yelled

"NO! These are not toys! Only adults can use these, you or I could have been hurt very badly! Do you understand me?".

Sniffling and nodding in compliance, I retreated to my room awaiting what further discourse would follow upon my father's finding out. Much to my surprise, I would not be met with the wrath I had envisioned erupting from my father. My father was a religious man and believed in discipline. He never liked to spank us, however, was not afraid to do so when warranted. This was a relief for me knowing what could have been. Much like a fire, he could be warm and comforting; yet if I became reckless, he would be quick to correct it.

My mother had begun to catch on that I could at times be a hellion. I was a very adventurous boy who loved to discover something new, always seeking a new adventure. I was quite the opposite of my sister who could carry a degree of sass with her. She was much the opposite when it came to being more composed and well behaved. My father had made a point of frequenting more check-ins while on the road to help reduce any more indiscretions.

Our days continued in a similar routine, at times we went on the road with our father to watch him perform. Other days we stayed the night with our mother at the dance studio. Despite the grueling past of my parents, we had always found ways to persevere in times of testing. Things had begun to finally stabilize as I adapted to the new schedules of my parents. Isabelle and I had been well-taken care of despite the few occurrences of which I am sure to have given my mother and father a heart attack due to my curious young mind. It seemed, however, looking back now, that despite how well we thought we would have it; many trials would constantly play in the background of our lives. Hiding in the shadows; waiting for the most inopportune time to creep in to disrupt any prayer of normality.

In 1992, long before my mind could formulate much, my five-year-old sister was taken from the home. In the first of many discouraging and plaguing trials of our lives, the first allegation came to light. Not just from anyone, but rather, from familiar faces of the past that set in motion a series of events to dictate the direction of my upbringing for many years to come. After an unexpected visit from the Department of Human Services accompanied by law enforcement; they announced their intention of removing Isabelle from the home. Many grotesque statements were disclosed to local law enforcement. Allegations of my father molesting my sister. Not that molestation in any capacity isn't disgusting, however, these were stories that could only be formulated in a fashion as if George Romero or Steven King had fabricated them in a starlight fiction.

Vaginal penetration with a sword amongst one of the most abysmal claims. Repeated offenses of abuse both physical and emotional. However, despite all of it, my father soon found out the source of these false claims. Regardless of the claims, the truth was to be found. It was indeed found when it was disclosed that not only were these horrendously fabricated, but in addition, a gag order was placed on our grand-parents, the Pennington's, to never speak with us children again in conjunction with a restraining order.

During the investigation, which concluded within three days, my sister had been removed from the home. She was placed temporarily with a foster family to await the conclusion of the allegations made. After three days my sister returned home with the traumatic events remaining only to scar her for years to come. The disruption imposed on her healthy young mind would be found to be created by none other than my mothers mom and dad,

Bill and Patty Pennington. Having been disconnected relationally some years ago, they could not let go of the fact that their daughter Lily had been swept away from them by my father. They no longer had the control they once possessed over her. In an effort to victimize John, they knew where to strike to induce the most pain. Break the family dynamic.

Yet again, we attempted to live out a normal life. That is, with counseling now added into the mixture. I, only being three-years-old at the time can only remember fragments of those days. We attempted for a while to retain normality following an instance such as this. But, how much rewiring would it take to forget these terrible things? Though the gag order was in place, no ramification ever came to the Pennington's when the truth was found out and all of the charges were dismissed by the court. Our family would have to try and find a new normal, my father could never truly obtain closeness to his children again in fear of another attack. He would always be certain to fight for us, but the emotions quickly faded as he had to keep affection at a distance.

This continued for some time. That is until I first learned of the full curse of the Kranz family name. It was 1994 and my sister and I accompanied our mother to her studio just like any other time. My father was on the road, and our mother directed us to stay upstairs while she retrieved some equipment from the studio's basement for a banquet to be held later that evening. Little did we know, that was the last day we would see our mother or father.

As we played in the upstairs ballroom running through the halls, we found ourselves picked up by two familiar faces. Taken, against our mother and father's knowledge, against our will. Not knowing how long until we could feel a warm embrace of love and comfort. It was our first descent into the pits of Hell. The first trial where we learned to grow and shape our worlds for years to come.

# The Descent

The few memories that flow through my head when I reminisce on the events of that day are the stale smell of spirits. Isabelle and me running up the old creaky wooden stairs and entering a small bar room. Round tables and chairs filled the floor with a long bar table stretching across the rear of the room. Bottles lined the wall with different pull tabs and shiny glass cups. Isabelle and me played tag in the bar of the dance studio as the lights were out and the rooms were empty. As we ran back and forth, the echoes of our footsteps clattering through the empty and lifeless ballroom could be heard throughout the studio. Suddenly, we were stopped near the iron heating vent at the top of the stairs. This walkway served as a gateway between the ballroom dance floor and the bar. This was where two familiar faces peered down at us with a stale, awkward, almost forced smile creeping across their faces. It was our grandma and grandpa Pennington.

They looked at us with an unconvincingly forged greeting.

"Hey babies! Your mom told us to pick you up. We're going to take you with us for a little while." They exclaimed.

Little to our knowledge, however, this was unknowing to our father and mother. For us this was nothing concerning. Though we had experienced the fallout and travesties of the disruption in recent years, our parents did well to keep us closed off to the legalities. They never spoke ill of our grand-parents and what they had done, in fact, they never spoke of them at all. After the first invasion of chaos when Isabelle was first removed, to our knowledge, they just stopped showing up.

Some time elapsed that we stayed at their house. Days had passed that we hadn't seen or heard from our parents. Homesickness began to set in. Though questions of their return would be raised by our inquiring minds, just as quickly would they be brushed to the side. The days were vague, and not much can be remembered during that short duration stay. Whether or not it was subconscious protection, or just too far distant from my mind, I may never know. The day suddenly came to a stop when it was interrupted by one of my most vivid and clear memories. The first trial I endured as a child. It was the first step down the relentless rabbit hole of my dark story.

You see, at the time, to us, it did not appear as abnormal as it would be to a more matured mind. It was just a weekend away with our grand-parents. Gag-orders and restraining orders didn't mean a thing to us at the time. We never would have given it a second thought. Not knowing how long it would last had never passed through our young minds. It didn't become abnormal until the following day.

Late into the evening while sitting in a room my sister and I would be abruptly awoken. Within moments, red and blue auras beamed through the windows. Flickering and reflecting off of the windows illuminating the room and the yard. Hours away from the solitude of our home men and women in uniforms surrounded the home. Within moments a loud crash and pounding could be heard as the front door was breached. Officers flooding in single file. Screaming and yelling echoed through the recently quiet home as it filled with the task force.

The officers came through the door, assuring us that we were safe now. My grandmother frantically argued her reasoning with the police.

"We had to remove them," She began "It wasn't safe for them there! Their father was doing horrendous things to them. We just needed to save them." She argued.

A strange lady emerged shortly after with some men in uniform with a badge and a gun. The officers separated us from our grandparents while the seemingly nice lady had us come with her. Yet again, another person exclaiming that we will be going to stay somewhere else for a short while. "Short" I guess was contingent on which side of hell we were on. Soon enough we found ourselves landed only a few blocks away with our "new" parents. The ones we were told would be safer for us.

Even though it had been two years since the previous allegations, the state did not dare take any chance of so easily dismissing the claims of our safety being jeopardized. Having to take all things into account, the state decided it would be best to launch a full fledge investigation. This would dive deep into the lives of my father, mother, and our grandparents. For Isabelle and I, this unfortunately meant we could not return home until a decision was made by the state.

When we arrived at the new home, as much as I try to

recall the accuracy of my first impression, I cannot help but presume it was dark and gloomy. Perhaps as if the world decided it was this day it was going to shit on me. This seemed to be a recurring theme throughout my story. Per the new norm, once we arrived we were greeted by an older couple. Much older than our mother and father. Certainly not as beautiful or handsome as the latter. It became ironic how many forced greetings we received over these last few months. Each adult claiming such a pleasure to meet us and what wonders surely awaited our young fragile minds.

Apparently, the State didn't think my sister was good enough, so they paired us with a family that wanted to offer us two more brothers and a sister. This was, the "foster family", exciting right? All seemed well enough as we settled into our new home. After a few weeks of attempting to adjust to our new surroundings the crying became less and less as Isabelle and I learned to rely on one another. We were it. She clung to me and became my protector. She made sure I was taken care of, dressed, and as happy as we could try to be. She always looked out for me. Even though we were only two years apart, she always made sure to mature much faster to ensure we were safe.

Reflecting back even now, this was probably the first time I had to attune myself to the wearing of different masks. Constantly having to adapt to new environments. It was our beginning to survival training, be it a curse or a blessing, we were groomed at an early age to learn to survive on our own. This in turn also created our hesitancy to be able to trust.

Frequently a strange lady came to meet with us. She

asked us all of these strange questions about our real mother and father. She always became very upset when we didn't answer her questions right though. Even if we told the truth, she insisted we were lying. She asked us if our mother or father had ever touched us in private places, or hurt us with their hands? Every time we answered, however, it was never a good enough answer. One time she grew so angry that she yelled at me.

"You better get used to your new home, because your father is going to get the electric chair and burn in hell!" She roared.

I was terrified. I loved my father and couldn't understand why anyone would want to hurt him? It became very confusing at times, almost as if it were a game to them. On occasion, they brought us candy or treats if we said stuff they wanted to hear. Through leading questions and probed remarks, we could occasionally appease them. That was probably one of the few refreshments we could embrace during these times. I mean, if it is just a game, why not take the treats?

The year that felt like a lifetime led to many unanswered questions. What did we do to deserve this? Why weren't we good enough? Even at a young age, it pressured us to question the essence of our worth in this world. Being moved like currency and thrown around like rag dolls, constantly being neglected by those who were supposed to protect us. This home would be what would shape us or break us.

It felt like a lifetime that we grew with our new family. I remember they always had input on how I should dress and look. My hair wasn't good enough the way I had it so they decided I should grow it differently. Then again, it was the nineties, so who cared if I had a rattail for a hairdo and some classy hand me down clothes? I looked like a child from The Hills Have Eyes. Not all of it was bad though. They did let us play video games from time to time, and if I got too loud or rambunctious towards the video game, I earned a time out here and there in the corner. Eventually, however, the corner wasn't enough. If I was too loud, or too hyper they hit me, it wasn't abuse, it was discipline. It was to just make sure I listened the next time.

Our foster dad would get angry too, but no one ever hit him. He did most of that himself. When he would get upset he went into the kitchen and started yelling as he repeatedly slammed his head into the refrigerator. "THUD", "THUD", "THUD," the refrigerator rocked back and forth across the laminate flooring while his head connected with the door. I guess I never gathered if it was something else, or perhaps he just really didn't like that refrigerator? It would have been more satisfying if he instead chose a lit stove or a brick. This grew to be our near-daily routine.

One day Isabelle had just had her hair beautifully braided into pigtails on either side. She felt like a princess. She was excited and didn't hesitate to flaunt her stylish new look. When our foster father returned home from the grocery store, he had many bags that were sprawled across the kitchen floor. Our new parents asked my sister to help put the groceries away, and as such, she obliged.

She grabbed the items from the bags and began placing them in the various spots throughout the kitchen. In doing so she came across a bag with canned goods in it. She reached down and began placing them on the shelves one by one. That was until, of course, the new parents weren't satisfied with her attempt to help. In a fit of discontent, the new mom grabbed Isabelle by her beautiful braids and flung her about the kitchen floor.

"Why can't you do anything right." The woman screamed.

My previously glimmering sister, my protector, laid battered and broken on the kitchen floor. Day by day it seemed another instance laid claim to any hope of salvation and peace. We couldn't do anything right. Not for our mother and father, not our foster mom and dad, and not for the strange lady. This truly was Hell, and we were defeated. Helpless. Worst of all, I was so small. I couldn't do anything to help my sister who had been so strong, willing, and able to always ensure my safety.

For the first few times it was terrifying. It was completely opposite of the emotional restraint our parents had. If this was safer than home, I guess I wouldn't know what normal was anymore. We certainly felt safer at home. After a few times, however, we began to adapt to it. The down side was, it showed me just how much I would have to control my emotions to not feel broken down. This is what strong was right? This four-year-old me had to quickly learn to grow up. I couldn't let the circumstances break me, or my sister.

It wasn't until a year later the disclosure of why we had to endure this pain came to light. During the time of our leisurely stay at our new parents, my father found himself pacing the house day in and day out pondering in despair. Wondering how to put his brilliant mind to use to bring us home. One day while rummaging through the empty house; lifeless and absent of his children's laughter, he stumbled upon a heartbreaking note that changed the course of this blind-siding blow to our family. For a year he was puzzled as to what provoked our ill-minded grand-parents to remove us? Why would anyone want to take their children away? After the death of two children already, losing David and Isabelle would add another equal blow; laying waste to any hopes of finding happiness.

That was until he found the letter. This letter was in a familiar finesse, a once loved one's handwriting, written to our grandparents. The one written by our mother, against my father's knowledge, instructing the Pennington's to take us away.

After the loss of two sons and the rough upbringing our mother had endured with her father, her mental status began to deteriorate. Despite the many psychological evaluations and the eventual diagnoses of Munchhausen's By-Proxy. A disorder that a caregiver, in our case; our mother imposed on Isabelle. A disorder that alleged Isabelle had a supposed illness or danger; such as being sexually abused. Because of this, the Pennington's could not bear to allow our father to keep us. Their abuse could not end with our mother, they needed to continually assert control over her through us. Passed down from her parents, as if a tradition, she now passed her agony on to us. This was why we had to endure this pain.

For fourteen months the abuse of the foster family and the State continued. Day in and day out. Until finally one day someone's prayer was answered. We were finally able to return home. Mother and father came and picked us up from a weird area that had all of these toys and board games. Our backpacks were filled with clothes and belongings. When they entered the room, without hesitation, we sprung towards them with our smiles touching ear to ear. The world around us faded out honing in on nothing other than the long-desired warm embrace of a loving touch. A feeling of sanctity and comfort. Our world that had grown so dark, decided finally to let up. The sun was able to shine through and give us a glimpse of hope to a normal family once again.

# The House of Cards

It was 1995, sometime after my sixth birthday. It was sunny and warm with the sun shining brighter than any day I could recall in recent months. Much had changed since our time away from our mother and father. By this time our parents had found a new house, not an apartment, but a house. It was a two-bedroom home in the northeastern outskirts of South Bend. We were just a few blocks away from the University of Notre Dame. It was white with a backyard of our own in Harters Heights. We had a neighbor on one side of us and an alleyway that separated us on the other. This was it, we finally could get back to the semi-partridge family that we wanted. At least that is what we thought we had.

After our return home, things had changed, not just with where we lived, but mother was different too. She always seemed tired, or confused. She spent a lot more time at her dance studio and the evenings lasted until the next morning at times. My father had stepped away from the role of Burger mascot for McDonald's and returned to spend more time at home. He had returned to school to work on his Associates in Accounting and performed magic with some clown gigs thrown in on the side. He picked up a job third shift at a nearby hotel so he could be sure to be home in time to get us up and dressed for school, catch a few hours of sleep, be there for us when we got home, and repeat his schedule. It was a daunting, tiring schedule for him, I'm sure of it. However, while attempting to hold his family together, the looming fear of what his beloved wife was now capable of could not escape his mind. Despite his dreary efforts, he was always sure we were taken care of.

Eventually, we had a new babysitter that would help around the house during the day. Our mother continued her previous trend of sleeping during the day with minimal involvement. She would frequent her promises of grand plans to go do things as a family. Each one ending with a "when I get home we can go to the movies!", or "we can go to the park, I just have some stuff to finish up at the dance studio." Each time our hopes would grow, and just as quickly they would fade with every broken promise. Day in and day out we knew mother was becoming different. She became someone we no longer knew.

After countless efforts of trying to get his wife help, each time she would attend therapy and be forced to face her deteriorating mental-wellbeing, she would quickly retreat. Each retreat devolved into a harder push that it wasn't her that needed help, rather, the therapists just didn't know how to do their job. Despite the efforts, my father felt helpless. Many diagnoses of bipolar disorder would come to the discussion in sessions, and each diagnoses further drove her into believing the therapists were the crazy ones. Though not her fault, my father was not equipped to know how to handle this.

We returned home from a day of errands with our

father. Mother had been at the dance studio all day and was dropped off shortly after our arrival. We walked through our front door passing through the living room, as Isabelle and I took our belongings to our room. My sister and I shared a room in the front corner of the home. We had a bunk-bed that fit snug in the corner of the room between two windows. I slept on the top bunk while my sister took the bottom. I had a plastic ninja turtle tent that I could retreat to for my imaginary adventures of being part of the crew with Donatello, Raphael, Leonardo, and Michaelangelo that rested near the closet of our toy ridden floor. We had finished our evening of playing after dinner when our father prepared us for bed. We picked our toys up and were tucked in. We drifted off to sleep just like any other night would have it.

I don't recall the time, I just recall the moon shining brightly through our window; reflecting off the hardwood floors. Isabelle and I suddenly awoke. Startled by the screams of our mother as she barged through our door, sprinting into our room naked and screaming.

"KIDS! QUICK! THE DEMONS ARE COMING TO GET US!" She Shouted "YOU NEED TO JUMP OUT OF THE WINDOW! QUICK! JUMP!"

Not far behind, our father rushed into our room after our delusional and paranoid mother who was shouting at us. Quickly wrapping his arms around her as she flailed and screamed, he brought her to the floor insisting she needed to calm down. Many moments elapsed before she was able to gather some of her senses and calm down. As they wrestled on the floor, eventually her manic episode subsided. Following the event, he helped mother off the floor. He escorted her back to the bedroom across the hall and tucked her back into their wood-framed water bed where she passed out.

Our father returned to our room to comfort us from the traumatic scene we had just witnessed. He turned the lights back down and tucked us back into bed. Sitting for a moment on the edge of the bottom bed he explained,

"Your mother is just not feeling very well." All the while assuring us that everything would be okay.

After the many episodes we had experienced from the foster care family and the State, we became fairly acclimated to harsh treatment from caregivers. Never from our mother and father though. This became a memory that has been forever forged into my mind. The beautiful woman that had birthed us and cared for us was gone. At that moment fear overcame us. We didn't know who it was coming into our room, but it certainly was not our mother. We were too young to understand. We were unaware of the letter our mother had written to her parents, so we never had any reason to concern ourselves with her intentions of caring for us.

Though this was the only occurrence we would face in this capacity, the change in our mother was forever present. Days came and went where at times she wouldn't return home at all. I recall several times we were promised a family night out to go see a movie at the local cinema, however, we only had one car. My mother would frequently take it; explaining she would be right back.

"I just have a quick errand to run." She would say.

My father, sister, and me would wait; and as the time elapsed it became despairingly evident that she was not returning. Our father would gather our clothes and jackets and we took to the streets in the evening to always try and fulfill the broken promises of our mother. We journeyed down the streets as the nightfall approached, at times walking several miles to embark on playtime at the park, or a late-night movie. This continued for nearly a year.

My birthday arrived and I remember waking up that morning. My mother entered the living room as I sat on the couch watching my cartoons. She looked beautiful. Her makeup was all done with her vibrantly red lipstick, gold hoops that freely dangled from her ears. A fresh perfume flowed off her dress and created a warm vibe of comfort. She leaned down over the couch, giving me a hug and a kiss on the cheek as she wished me a happy birthday.

"Happy birthday buddy! I just have to go to work for a little bit. When I come home, how about I bring you a happy meal?" She said.

I couldn't be more excited. I was going to get a happy meal and an evening with my mother. Much to my surprise, however, I would find that just as in every other instance, it was not going to be. Waiting at home anxiously, checking out the window while the day progressed, the night drew nearer as my eyes filled with tears. Heavy and heartbroken, our mother didn't return.

As the ever-changing instances progressed, consuming our mother day by day, the woman we once knew and loved dissipated slowly before our eyes. After much abandonment and the continual episodes, Isabelle had enough. She looked to our father with weary, broken, teary eyes. Distraught and filled with discontent she spoke to our father,

"Daddy, why can't mommy just die?"

Disturbed by this remark from his eight-year-old daughter, but ever evident that the woman he once fell in love with was no more. Our father knew this could no longer be the path for him and his children. It was time.

Once again finding ourselves lost and confused, we soon grew familiar with the absence of our mother. Each time progressing longer and longer. The final stage, however, was when she no longer returned home. They had come to endure the long talk with our father.

"Mom and Dad love you both very much!" He began.

"None of this is your fault, but mom and dad are not going to be living together anymore. You will still get to see us both, but things will be different for a little while."

A new day arose, however, this time we would not awake to a dazed mother. Sleepily confused, or urging to rush out the door. We would awake from our beds to begin walking past our parents' bedroom, dark and vacant. Trudging down the narrow hallway past the bathroom, past the dark kitchen, not even a drop to fall from a once frequented kitchen sink. Looking at the pictures draped on the wall as we passed, we emerged to the vacant living room. An empty couch sat in the middle of the room as the subtle taps of footsteps was the only greeting awaiting us. We entered as our reflection peered back at us from the blank television. Our father sat at the dining room table in silence. A home once filled with life once again sat empty in emotion.

Our world, just as the puzzle pieces began to form, was just as eager to fall apart. Like a house of cards, one by one they fell, crashing down around us. Was this all we had to look forward to?

# Trial & Heir

We spent weeks moving around as we re-adjusted to the life of a single father taking care of us. New people would come and go, often women hurrying out of the home as we awoke. It was a new life without our mother home every day. Our father, especially after the recent years, had taken on a role-model as a stern best friend and mentor. The emotional bonding and nurturing, however, remained at a distance. Between the many concerns of our mother's mental health, and lack of desire to address them; the courts decided our father was best suited as our primary caregiver. He was granted sole-custody of both Isabelle and me.

On occasion, we found ourselves frequenting my grandmother's home in Grand Rapids. Patricia was her name, grandma Pat for us; she was my father's mother. She was a sweet lady but had iron-clad determination. She would always spoil us any given opportunity. However, if you ever wronged her or her loved ones; it would be hell to pay! Like the saying would go, "Hell hath no fury like a woman scorned." Though the damage in our lives was not due to her love affair, however, someone attempted to hurt her family, her blood. She was a forgiving person, yet, she knew when too much was too much. That was one of the few traits we carried in our family. We only allowed ourselves to be hurt so much before we began to cut the toxicity out of our lives. She had become very good at that. She too was a single mother growing up. She always made sure that her children were taken care of. She was a strong-willed independent woman. I like to believe that her hard-working and moral compass is what was passed down our male side of the family. If nothing else, it could never be disputed that the Kranz' would always face adversity head-on, no matter how messy or small the odds would be for success. We weren't raised to quit.

Our uncle Fred lived with her. He too was very involved with our well-being growing up. Though our grandma Pat spoiled us, Fred was always sure to try and make us laugh. Especially after the loss of his two nephews, he always made a continued effort to be involved in our lives.

I can still remember the smell of stale cigarette smoke, and the yellow-tinted walls from the nicotine. The short furred carpet of the kitchen, and the dated appliances. Much of our time there was spent sitting in the living room with its slightly longer shag carpet on the floor in front of the TV watching our Saturday morning cartoons. A lamp rested on the table to the left of the living room entrance, gold in color with a rotary dial phone resting beside it. A long mirror sprawled across the wall above the couch, reflecting to the large window across the room giving a great view of my grandmother's bird feeders. Plants lined the far wall below the smaller window sill with a china cabinet filled with collectible salt and pepper shakers. Our grandma loved to collect the matched sets of human figurines. Anything else had no place in her collection. As a six-year-old boy, the adventures, nurturing, love, and safety were ever-present at our grandma's house. It would always emanate feelings of safety and comfort.

Our father wasn't much of a cook, so the lavish meals and frequent candies always managed to keep our attention when we visited. Sitting in front of the TV and watching shows on Nickelodeon that always managed to make them both twitch at the stupid humor that would be played, that in turn, Isabelle and I would adore. Hysterically laughing and mimicking whatever non-sense filled the screens; *Real Monsters, Ren and Stimpy, Rocco's Modern Life*, on occasion we would switch back to somewhat normal shows to give some sanity back to the weekend caretakers. *Hey Arnold*, or *Gulla Gulla Island*. My favorites were always, *Are You Afraid of The Dark* and *Goosebumps*. I loved the mystical mysteries of the tragedies that always had me gripping the arms of the fold-out kid's chairs we sat in. The ones that kept me on edge only to find the happy ending would always result in some twist of a further decline. It felt relate-able.

We were spoiled with toys and a large backyard. Our uncle built a swing set for us one summer to embark on new journeys. Space and activities such as this were a magical playground for any six-year-olds' adventurous mind. Even with the changes in my surroundings, I couldn't help but try and find the joy in the small things of life.

One Sunday afternoon while we were playing outside with our Uncle Fred, our father pulled into the driveway to pick us up to return home. We remained outside while he entered the home to greet our grandmother. He entered through the creaky door into the laundry room.

Walking past the upstairs walkway and into the old appliance kitchen. Through the sharply turned hall and into the living room just past the golden touch lamp and rotary dial phone. My grandmother was sitting in her claimed seat to the right with her reclining couch.

"Hey ma!" My father said in a soft greeting manner. Brushing his hand through his hair and taking a seat below the long mirror on the couch. *Sigh* "How were the kids this weekend?" He inquired.

"They were fine" She began, "This is the first time I have seen them this happy. Since the separation that is. How are you doing?".

My father again let out a brief sigh while nodding in compliance.

"I'm fine," he said while running his hand through his hair again.

"This is just so much to try and take on. I don't know where I would be without you and Fred. I'm just always so tired."

"You would be a little less tired if you spent less time with those girls you keep chasing!" Pat replied sarcastically.

My father let out a slight chuckle as a sly grin crept to one side of his face.

"Ya ma, I know. I'm just trying to find the right woman. Someone the kids can look up to instead of being ashamed of." He said.

"Lily just isn't right."

As my father looked to his mother he squinted in disgust, "You know the other day I brought the kids to Lily's for their visit. She turned us away!?" He began.

"The kids were in tears! Lily said she had a dance that

night and wasn't taking them. She even threatened to call the police if we didn't get off her property. Who does that to their kids?!" He ranted, growing more irritated as he reflected back on the incident.

"I told you I didn't like that woman, John," Pat replied tapping her foot on the fuzzy carpet.

My grandmother was never too fond of my mother. She merely tolerated her out of her love for her son, my father. After the many dramatic instances during their younger years, including them running away together, our mother's mental health and neglect of her kids never sat well with our grandma.

My father and grandma Pat looked to the walkway as the sound of a door creaked open. Children's feet could be heard stomping into the kitchen with typical chatter. Running through the doorway we greeted our father.

"DADDY!" We both exclaimed in unison. Fred following close behind them with a fresh stale scent of a recently smoked cigarette emitting from his jacket.

"Hey!" Fred said in a quirky voice, as he would always do while greeting one of us.

"Hey Fred," My father replied.

"Well, we better hit the road. We have a bit of a drive and I don't want the kids up too late. Grab your stuff kids and say goodbye to grandma Pat and Fred."

We gathered our belongings and gave our hugs to our grandmother and uncle Fred. Loading back into our car ready to embark on our two-hour drive back to Indiana.

Much of my life up until now had encapsulated insecurity and uncertainty. Though as hard as our father tried to keep normalcy in our lives, the instability remained. It seemed like the world that had the potential to offer so much had deteriorated to an unsafe place. We had moved frequently making it difficult to find and keep friends. The only stability we grew to rely on was our father, grandma Pat, and uncle Fred.

Time continued as such of the repetition of our father frequenting new women. We continued day in and day out wondering why we weren't good enough for our mother. Mother too had moved on to someone new. Jeff was his name. He was a stocky dark-haired man with glasses. Frequent in a T-shirt and sweat shorts. It didn't matter the time of year though; it was always shorts. The man was immune to the cold it seemed. My mother had moved into a small two-story duplex on the east side of town. It was a fairly run-down brick building where she resided on the bottom floor. At times she would find a way to fit us into her busy schedule. However, as history would have it, most of her time would be spent sleeping on the couch as Isabelle and I would entertain ourselves through puzzles and board games. Despite the lack of involvement, I still found myself heart-broken at the ever rapidly approaching, always too soon, departure of our time with her.

This was a confusing time in my life. Children around me always had the Partridge family I would adore on the television. Their mothers and fathers would laugh and joke; even endure hardships together equally abiding by a supporting structure. Why was ours so different? I grew to resent the normalcy of other families. How come their mother's loved them, but mine had no desire to claim me? Life seemed very unfair.

As the months went on, our father finally found a

woman he wanted to settle down with. Gemma was her name. She was a red-haired woman with glasses and covered in freckles. It was difficult at first trying to adjust to splitting our time with our father and this new family. She had three children of her own; Chuck, Mike, and Marge. Gemma always managed to try and make Isabelle and I feel accepted as one of her own though. Despite the rapidly changing family dynamic; having another boy in the home closer to my age awarded me the opportunity to bond with someone else. Chuck and I would find ourselves imaginary sword fighting, or playing hide and seek in the small stretch of woods that resided behind their apartment complex. My father had known her for years, it was now they decided to finally connect though.

This went on until 1997 when they married. Coincidentally, this would also be the year that two more brothers were added to the family tree. Just before my father and Gemma re-connecting, it appeared my father spent some extracurricular time re-connecting with another woman as well. That year Joseph and Harry were born. Joseph would be born from my father and a crazy, short-haired, John Travolta, Grease obsessed, college student; and Harry born from my father and Gemma. It was also this year, however, that we merged the Kranz and Werkema, families. Instead of having one sibling, it quickly grew to six children and two parents in a small two-bedroom apartment. Soon we found ourselves moving to the south suburbs of Grand Rapids into a small three-bedroom trailer just a few blocks from my grandma Pat's house.

It was tough re-adapting to a new family, in a new neighborhood, and new schools once again. Chuck and I spent the nights running through the trailer park awaiting the street lights to kick on to give the ever daunting signal that it was time for us to return home. Two seven-year-olds running around by themselves, what trouble could they get into? For the most part, we managed to get along with most of the kids in the neighborhood. That is at least the ones our age.

Chuck and I had grown a close bond to one another. Though we came from different families, we both had experienced hardships in our own ways in life. Since we were only several months apart, our interests aligned almost instantly. We were in the same grade, the same school, and the same sporting events. It allowed us to forget the blood bond, and form a brother bond.

One day Chuck and I went to go play down by the pond that was only two streets over from us. We went down and attempted to see what fish we could catch with our hands. Getting the mucky, green, slimy goop of the pond on us, we stepped in to see what luck would bless us that day. Seldom did it render results.

While attempting our native fishing skills, two older kids across the pond had apparently obtained a new wrist rocket. While picking up nearby pebbles and launching them through the water, Chuck and I became viable targets. As the first pebble whizzed past our ears striking the waters to our side, we quickly realized these were no longer unintended shots. Instead, it was us they were aiming for! Shot after shot, as the rocks would "ping" and "clank" off of the objects surrounding us from cars to trailer sidings; I suddenly found myself startled and in awe. Within moments I found myself gripping my chest and collapsing to the ground. Something had just knocked the wind clear out of me.

"This was it", I thought! "I'm dying!" Little did I know in my adolescent mind, it would just hurt like hell for the next few days. I grasped my chest while erupting in tears from the stinging of the rock. The rock that chose to decorate my body with pretty blue and purple marks, no larger than the size of a nickel. Within moments, our older step-brother Mike emerged from around the corner. Our hero. To his surprise he saw me laying on the ground, holding my chest in tears as adults began to walk nearer to us. With the crowd of adults growing, they began to approach, wondering what all of the noise was. Chuck quickly points Mike towards the kids with the wrist rocket,

"They hit David!" He yelled.

Not the slightest bit phased by the dainty pebbles; Mike quickly jumped to action taking off in pursuit. Now, Mike was only a few years older than us, however, he was a stocky and broad-shouldered young-man; almost as if a running back for an NFL team. Mike took off in chase grabbing a stick as he ran. The two kids saw this Goliath catching up to them ever quickly, as they turned to the woods and began to flee. All the while, they aimlessly fired more pebbles; now at Mike's body. As the pebbles ricochet off of Mike's broad body, he hardly flinched as his eyes were set to his target like a lion to its prey. He rapidly approached them, when he soon found himself stumbling. Just as with the infamous Newton's law, an object in motion, especially as big an object as he, certainly remains in motion. Unfortunately, that whole gravity thing took effect as well as he plummeted to the ground scraping his legs as if just dumping a Harley Davidson on asphalt.

Picking himself up and dusting himself off, he looked to find his targets had gotten away. He began to make his way back towards his two younger brothers, Chuck and me. When he returned to the pond he found that instead of just a few parents, two officers were now there with their notepads and cameras asking what had happened while taking a picture of my bare bruised chest.

Somehow we always managed to find ourselves getting in some sort of trouble. We frequently pressed our limits as the misfit family. One day we received our first checked out library book of "Scary Stories to Tell in the Dark", only to be accompanied by the audiotape that would haunt us the most! The following morning when our parents left for work, in one giant team of troubling adolescents, we looked to each other in agreement; we were going to skip school and listen to scary stories. As our parents left we began to set the mood by piling into our sister's small, compact, mobile home bedroom. We lined the windows with sheets and blankets to make it as dark as we were able to. As we turned the lights out, sat on the floor, and placed the cassette tape into our radio we began to listen to the story of the missing toe. Though, quickly we found that the scary stories were not the most terrifying part.

After nearly three stories, while our adrenaline and anxiety were at their peak, just before the final telling of the scary story; the bedroom door flew open as we all simul-taneously jumped to our feet and screamed. You would almost think it was our souls floating out of us as our parents stand in the doorway, very evidently displeased. Even as a young boy who loved adventures, disappointing parents was not part of the adventure. Our plan might have worked well if our parents hadn't decided to stop home only a short hour later after receiving a phone call from the school informing them of our absence. Despite the abrupt fear evoked from our parents, who were severely displeased, a loss of television and an early bedtime was all that would come from our disobedient act of truancy.

Our first two years after the divorce proved to be fairly normal. We embraced the large family. No barging into our bedrooms in the middle of the night telling us to jump out windows, or having concerns of someone taking us away to some faraway land from all we knew. Things were beginning to become normal again for us.

My father, as a good distraction from our previous encounters, and I'm sure as well to establish a lineage had begun to teach me how to perform some magic tricks myself. At eight years old he bought me my very first magic set. With a small, cheap, plastic set of cards; a few sponge balls, three plastic cups, and a rope. As much as I tried to learn different tricks and props, cards had always been my fascination.

My father being a stage performer helped me to learn showmanship, however, he had limited variation of card techniques. This I learned to be one of my greatest escapes at an older age from the continued attacks of my mother.

I knew my father was excited to share this large imprint of lineage with me, and I too as an escape from reality at times. It was always fun to learn and try new tricks. The teachers at school, however, did not find them as exciting as I did. After several complaints of playing during class and a few phone calls to my father regarding, "their son who was trying to escape from bicycle locks on the monkey bars"; my father felt it was time to set rules for his little aspiring Houdini.

It became a newfound passion. I loved learning new tricks. Standing in front of the mirror nearly daily I found myself astounding myself with a new move or sleight of hand technique that I would eagerly rush to the living room to show my father. His approval meant the world to me.

That was until life found its own way to continually pack a punch, leaving me speechless and breathless. I soon found that the Kranz curse would continue its pursuit. Only a few short years after my mother and father's separation we now began the new journey of endless court proceedings. This time to dispute who should claim rightful ownership of Isabelle and me. This became a frequent trend. It seemed as though every year we continued to do so. However, more and more it began to feel that instead of a genuine want of mine and Isabelle's presence, our mother wanted us as nothing more than the toy in the middle of the floor of a daycare. It wasn't that she wanted us, she just didn't want our father to have us. We were a trinket to be kept and sat on a shelf as a collectible porcelain doll. Something she could pull out to show how great she was while striking pain into the heart of our father. While strings trickled from our backs, leading up to the frivolous puppeteer hands of our mother; we were nothing more than marionettes in what became a lifelong battle between our father and mother.

For the next few years, we found ourselves in constant custody disputes. Regardless of the previous psychological evaluations, evidence that the kidnapping was formulated by our mother, and the genuine neglectful conduct from our mother that consistently granted my father continuous custody rights; her efforts were relentless. She had no care for the collateral damage that would ensue, as long as she won, that was all that mattered to her.

# Cutler Mansion

"**I** GOT IT!" I excitedly yelled while running across the soft grass.

Sprinting across the field on a fall evening, the white and black spotted ball tumbled across the damp grass. Children's screaming and cheers could be heard echoing through the trailer park. Our father, the cub scout leader, stood to the sidelines ensuring equal participation, watching with a whistle in hand as dozens of young men dashed across the field. Treating the ball as the last cookie in the kitchen, each team tirelessly ran towards the ball.

Chuck and I had been split up for the teams that evening. Even though Chuck and I were inseparable by this time, our drive for "being better than the other" applied greatly. Both determined in our competitiveness with one another, we sprinted back and forth, eyes on the target, that ball. The ball quickly found itself in Chuck and I's cross-hairs. We both locked on to it like an F14 fighter jet preparing to engage its target. Shutting out the world around us, adrenaline rushing through our veins as the cool air filled our tired lungs. Huffing and puffing with our rosy red cheeks, we found ourselves rapidly approaching the ball.

Preparing to make the game-winning goal; I prepared

to take my shot. I draw my leg back, without a second thought engaging the ball. Giving all of my efforts, I go for it. Awaiting the glorious cheers of my teammates, I go to kick the shot of the evening! Except, that shot would not be had. As I rushed to the ball and gave that hopeful kick, instead of glorious cheers and yelling, I would instead hear the loud, agonizing scream and snap bounding from my now pulsating kneecap. Not paying attention, Chuck and I both kicked at the same time. However, his slightly longer legs gave him the advantage as it swipes past the ball and connects with my knee cap. Dropping to the ground, grasping my now limp and intensely painful knee, my father blows the whistle.

My step-mother Gemma, who was a Licensed Practical Nurse, approached me to take a look at what all of the fuss was about. She looked down to my knee, took a kneel, and grasped both sides of my leg. I flinched and let out a roar as she touched both sides of the knee.

"It doesn't look broken, probably just bruised. Quit being a baby, just get up and walk home. We will take a look at it later." She scoffed.

I wiped my eyes and struggled to my feet with the assistance of my father and step-mother. Wobbling to my feet I limped slowly down the darkened road. The street lights now guiding our path down the two small mobile home park blocks. We finally approached the steps to the much-desired resting spot for my "bruised leg". Step by step grunting and panting, I made my way through the front door. As the night passed, I found myself groaning and whimpering as the pain endured from the rough blow to my knee would not subside. No amount of Tylenol seemed to offer any remedy. I awoke the next morning and hobbled to school. Again, only to be haunted by the pain, throbbing through not just my knee anymore, but down my whole leg. Three days passed until finally, the school had decided I should not continue until a doctor had cleared me to be back at school. The once slightly bruised and swollen leg had now ballooned into a near softball-sized kneecap. After being collected by my step-mother and father, they had finally concurred with the decision of the school to take me to the hospital to be evaluated.

"It's broken," The doctor said with certainty. Pinning the x-rays to the board in front of us.

My parents both stared blankly and shocked as the words slipped from the doctor's mouth so nonchalant. They both looked to one another in awe.

"How did we miss this?" They both silently whispered to one another.

"He will need surgery. It appears he has chipped a portion of the patella. We will have to surgically remove the portion and it may require a few screws." The doctor continued as money signs began flashing atop Gemma and John's mind. Both quickly became haunted at the thought of surgery.

Without hesitation, they agreed with the doctor's decision of the surgery. Understanding fully, I would not be returning home with my parents that evening; I was to be admitted to the hospital waiting to go under the shiny scalpel. As the time grew nearer, I found myself lying in a bed in a bright white room. Nurses and the doctor surrounded me with a calming voice.

"What flavor candy do you like?" The nurse began as she rummaged through a drawer.

"We have Strawberry, Cherry, Grape." She continued.

"I like strawberry!" I excitedly replied.

"Ok, strawberry it is dear." with a warm smile as she pulled a gelatin packet out of the cabinet drawer.

"We are going to put this mask on you, and you tell us when you begin to taste or smell the strawberry" she requested.

The nurse applied the clear plastic device encapsulating my nose and mouth as the air began blowing towards my nose and mouth. The sweet smell of strawberry began filling my senses as the nurse began asking me to start counting from ten to one slowly.

"Ten, nine, eight..." Though I tried my hardest, I was unable to complete the simple task as the world around me began fading to black.

What felt like mere moments had elapsed, I awoke in a different room. This time with a television in front of me, a table to the side of the bed with food decorating a white plate and a plastic cover. My parents sat in a chair to the right of me in the corner as my father began to stand as if he had been waiting years to greet me from a deep sleep.

"Hey bud, how are you feeling?" He began.

Attempting to fully open my eyes, I felt groggy and sluggish, still trying to comprehend what had happened, I attempted to sit up as a sudden sharp pain darted down my left knee.

"OW!" I shrieked. Uncovering my leg to reveal the source of the pain.

"Careful David, just take it easy. Don't try and get up."

The man in the white jacket began.

"You just came out of surgery. We had to cut your leg open to help fix where your bone was broken. It is all fixed, but now you will need to rest for a few weeks so it can get strong again." The doctor finished.

"I'm hungry" I replied.

My father, asking the doctor if it is okay for me to eat begins to reach for the tray of cooked carrots, peas, mashed potatoes, and chicken resting beside my bed.

"If he feels up to it, there is no reason he cannot" the doctor replies.

My father grabbed the tray placing it on my lap as he retrieved the utensils from the table next to where it had rested.

After a few small bites, feeling ravenous and starving my eyes widened in excitement.

"This is so good! We never eat like this at home!" I exclaimed, leaving little time between bites for breathing.

Simultaneously both parents looked to me, darting their eyes with a slight scowl and a forced chuckle.

We were clearly not underfed in our house, I had just not had a large repertoire of compliments in my freshly foggy mind. What better way to compliment someone than praise their food as better than your parents? Reflecting back now, perhaps I did a poor job explaining my gratitude.

Less than a night passed when I was finally cleared to go home. Late into the evening, the doctors discharged me, giving full freedom back to me as I prepared to head back home with my parents. Not without parting gifts of course. I began to transition off of the hospital bed, my leg freshly decorated with a blue foam cast and bright white Velcro straps to hold it in place. Two metal sticks with padding on top were given to me to help maintain my balance as I was instructed to keep as much weight off of my leg as possible for the next several weeks. Adjusting to my new temporary legs, I rested the crutches beneath my arms to pivot into the wheelchair waiting for me next to the bed. Staff wheeled me through the halls of the hospital to the main entrance where my father had been waiting with the car. John and Gemma helped me transition from the wheelchair to the car before resting my new crutches to my side.

After arriving home I was able to lay on the couch since I was not able to climb the ladder leading me to a comfortable bed I was previously acquainted with. The night felt like it would last forever. I twisted and turned all night in pain; endlessly attempting to find a comfortable position to reside.

Many weeks had passed and I was finally becoming more proficient with the crutches. Trying to gain strength as the doctor had instructed. It was nearing the year 2000. While the world around us was in fear of an imaginary apocalypse of Y2K, my father managed to land a new job as an accountant at Pine Rest, while simultaneously starting up his own computer business. Pine Rest was a mental health facility just a few blocks from our trailer park.

As a rapidly expanding family, we quickly outgrew the three-bedroom trailer that we all managed to pack into like a child's closet. With six children in the home and another one on the way, our three-bedroom trailer was no longer sufficient for our family of soon to be nine. My father spoke with the property owners and managed to strike a deal to rent out what was called The Old Cutler Mansion. It was right across the street from the notorious mental health campus. It was a sixteen bedroom, three-floor brick mansion. Grey in color with a fire escape trailing from the side of the house to the third-floor lookout, it was a sight to be had as a young ten-year-old boy. It almost reminded me of the House on Haunted Hill. There were several acres of woods behind the house with trails we could run through, that is if we didn't manage to get lost in the creepy old house we had just moved into. The only thing that horrified me from the beginning was the idea of having to hobble up so many stairs with a bunk leg. It was indeed going to be a challenge, but sure enough, it would certainly strengthen my leg, or my arms at the very least from all of the stairs. Crutches and stairs were not my best of friends.

I still remember the first day we began to move in. One of the maintenance workers from the campus was walking by.

"Are you the new tenants?" He asked us inquisitively.

My father, with his typical show voice, replied, "We are! How are you doing today?"

"Good" he began with a sly smirk slowly crossing his face, "have you guys heard the stories of what you're moving into?"

Nodding with a look of confusion John responds "I have not. It's not going to fall apart on us is it?" My father replied, slightly chuckling in what can be heard as a forced effort.

Though we weren't hurting financially, any thought of

having to pour money into a failing home while feeding six kids was not at the top of the striving goal list.

"The place is haunted! We always hear weird noises, lights turning on and off, people walking past the windows. The strange part is, the home has been vacant for years. Used to be the original psychiatric hospital." The man replied.

As a family who grew up in show business and performing magic, my father slightly rolled his eyes letting out yet another forced chuckle. "Ahh okay, thanks for the heads up! Have a good one!" He replied, looking to me while condescendingly rolling his eyes in disbelief of the man's claims.

Disregarding the man's statement, my father turned back to the moving van and continued unloading items and boxes from the back.

Despite the eerie aura the house presented in of itself as a historical landmark for the small town of Cutlerville, we had yet to be gifted by any visits of the paranormal promises the maintenance man had made before our first night's stay. Though, it did always give us an uneasy vibe. Walking up the stairs of the porch we entered through the foyer. Red carpet sprawled the length of the foyer trailing into the dining room that lay behind two glass swinging doors. It was remarkable! A coat rack greeted anyone who entered the home with beautiful wood trim and crown molding. A green room back porch rest just to the far end of the dining room giving a show to a breathtaking backyard. We began carrying items through the dining room and followed the twists and turns through the first floor of this remarkable castle.

Passing down the narrow hallway, a large, creaky wooden door led us into the two-stall bathroom. That's right, stalls! It felt like we had our own business building! We continued past and began to set our belongings in the first-floor living room just to expedite the process of unloading the vehicles. The living room had a pearly white fluffy carpet, spanning the whole length of the house. Glass display cabinets held old wooden rocking chairs and other antique displays of the original owners of the mansion. Black and white photos decorated the walls of a family that disturbingly resembled our own. A family of ten sat in the black and white photos absent of any sign of emotion. I never liked those photos. Even though I didn't believe in ghosts, they still gave me the creeps!

Offering as much help as I could, balancing on two crutches, I attempted to offer whatever support I could to finish moving boxes and items into the home so we could be free to roam and lay claim to our room. A luxury we were never previously afforded due to the large size of our family and limited space available. Night drew nearer as we finally finished packing the beautiful living room with all of our belongings. It was astonishing that our previous homes belongings could all fit in a single room of our new home. Our parents directing us, "We will order some pizza for tonight, why don't you guys go pick out your rooms. The second floor is off-limits for bedrooms, but you can all pick one on the third floor!" They said as they disappeared upstairs.

Within moments of the release through the castle, Mike, Marge, Chuck, and Isabelle all rushed through the home as if starring on an amazing race. Noise was echoed through the home as laughter and bantering could be heard with every clunk and thud of them rushing up the stairs. Still moderately crippled I would be found slowly shuffling across the red-carpeted floor on my crutches, as if tortoise and the hare, I was clearly the tortoise in this race.

Wandering through the home I came up to the long, never-ending stairwell that would ascend to the second floor. Stair by stair, I climbed, crutches in hand as they creaked with every precise step of crutch and foot. Stiff legged, counting as I went I made progress up the twenty-four step stairwell. Finally reaching the top to yet another bathroom at the head of the stairs. Again, a wooden swinging door emerged to yet another two-stall bathroom with two stand up showers. We all could have our own bathroom pretty much! Not sure which direction to go I looked to the right to find yet another room, a small playroom perhaps that emerged into another living room. Two living rooms! I was in shock. We had always managed to make do with one, what on earth would we need with two?

Turning back, I found a drinking fountain to the top left of the stairway in surprisingly good working order. That's right, our very own drinking fountain. It was incredible. Taking a short stop to refresh me with the cold water from the fountain, I continued past the wooden rails that lined the second-floor hallway to keep one from falling to their demise down the long drop to the first floor. Passing by the mirror that spanned the length of the wall and approaching another stairwell. This one, fortunately for me, was much shorter than the first. However, it was much steeper. Thankful to have my own bedroom, I was still less than thrilled to have to climb a mountain daily under my current circumstances to get to my room.

A glass door waited at the top of the mountainous stairwell that had a different creak than the previous doors. It was very distinct as it emerged on the third floor. "Creeeaakkk" I can still envision it now. A bedroom waiting with my name on it at the top of the stairs. "Ahh yes," I thought to myself, "if I take this room, I won't have to carry stuff as far and can finally rest my leg!" I could see the excitement in each of the other sibling's eyes as they panned in and out of each of the five available rooms upstairs. Isabelle, glowing like I had not seen in years, picked the room just to the left of mine across the hall. Oddly shaped, it had its own fire escape exit onto a beautiful octagon shaped walkout balcony. Though Isabelle and I had not been as close as we were prior to the new marriage of our father and Gemma, we still genuinely cared about one another's happiness. Knowing where we came from, each one of us carrying our own baggage from previous years of neglect, abandonment, and let down; we felt like royalty that day. We became kings and queens of our own paradise in a world that had beaten us down so hard.

Approaching the top of the twenty-four step stairwell one evening, I could hear yelling echo through the mansion.

"You have got to be fucking kidding me-" Gemma roared.

She continued through the second floor of the house, stomping and huffing with every step.

"He is your son, fuck Jeff's pager, it's your weekend with him!" She continued.

I finished climbing the stairs as fury could be seen flowing from Gemma's mouth as she wandered into hers and my father's bedroom slamming the door. I walked past the bedroom at the top of the stairs, past the drinking fountain approaching their heavy wooden door. I began to ball my fist in preparation to knock on the heavy door.

By this time, we had been several years past the divorce of my mother and father. After recurring cases of being dragged into court, what felt like monthly, the current order stood that my sister and I had visitation with my mother bi-weekly on the weekends. Since it was so close to my surgery, however, we had to make some adjustments to the prior agreement. Because of the surgery, the doctors were concerned of travel too soon since the prolonged duration of travel could potentially put me at risk for unnecessary clotting. Though my leg was not my mother's fault, it certainly gave her reason to once again refuse to see her children.

My hand slowly approached the door to make a connection for the first knock, before I could though, it rapidly swung open to a livid, red-haired, red-faced Gemma yelling, "No, you can tell him you worthless cun-" she began, surprised to see me standing before her.

Extending the white cordless phone in her hand towards me,

"Here David, it's your mother. She would like to tell you something." She said with a curled lip as she turned to storm back into her bedroom.

Grabbing the phone from Gemma's hand I lit up with excitement,

"Hi, mom!" I exclaimed.

"Hey baby, how are you?" My mother asked.

"Good, are you still going to come to see me this weekend?" I inquired.

"Well, unfortunately, I can't Hunny. Jeff's pager for the fire department won't reach that far, so we are unable to make it this weekend." She began.

After a few weeks of depravity from my mother, my eyes slowly began to fill with tears as the oh so familiar feeling encased my body.

"Well, why can't Jeff just stay home and you come to see me?" I asked, sniffling.

"I'm sorry baby, I just can't." Mother replied.

My previously controlled emotion began to slowly erupt as I could no longer contain my feelings of missing my mother. Struggling to form a coherent sentence Gemma walked up behind me and snatched the phone from my hand.

"Your son is sitting here crying, begging you to come up to see him. What the hell is wrong with you? Why would we even humor more visits when you can't even make the ones that are set for you!" She screamed.

Now caught in what felt like the middle of the storm; I no longer was able to contain myself. I retreated to the only safe space I knew for myself. My bedroom. Barely able to see where I was limping to I just began to walk. Up the short narrow creaky stairs. Through the noisy glass door and to my room I went, closing the door behind me. Every instance that these would occur, I could not help but wonder, what was wrong with me? Why did our mother never want anything to do with us? Did she not love us? Were we no longer important to her? Isabelle never seemed phased by the negligent actions of our absent mother. Regardless of her views, she still managed to maintain her intent of being my protector. She would complain, but always was sure much like our father to keep my spirits high in sharing my excitement. I never was good at being angry. With each scar my mother left on me mentally, I would just as quickly return to her like a loyal dog excited to see its owner. I loved her dearly, however, I could never understand why she couldn't love me back. Isabelle had caught on much more quickly than I.

Many weeks had passed when I was finally given the news that my leg was healed and I was cleared to remove the itchy blue cast. This also meant I was able to continue visits with my mother. Not having to worry about whether or not my mother would come to us, I could now go to her. Friday had quickly approached as we were now able to continue our first visit with our mother in weeks. Isabelle and I packed our bags and prepared for our weekend away with our mother and Jeff. We loaded into the family van and made our way south of Kalamazoo. We met in a small town at a McDonald's parking lot right across the street from a gas station where the exchange took place.

Any other time we would load our bags up in Jeff's car and make our way to Indiana where we would reside for the remainder of the weekend. This weekend, however, was different. Isabelle, upset at our mother, had decided she was not going to speak with her at all that weekend. Before we left the parking lot Isabelle made her way into the McDonald's lobby to use the bathroom where our mother trailed closely behind. Jeff and me taking this same opportunity as well to use the restroom.

After going to the bathroom we decided to wait in the lobby for the other two, Isabelle and my mother. Moments had gone by where still; they had not emerged from the restroom. As we waited something had caught our attention, as well as the attention of the other patrons sitting at their tables eating. Their pleasant evening of a meal was abruptly disturbed by screaming and shouting erupting from the women's bathroom. The screaming and shouting eventually turned to cries as Isabelle would yell,

"STOP! YOU'RE HURTING ME!".

Finally, one of the patrons had enough. Concerned with my sister's well-being, the older woman who was eating a meal at the table near the door entered the bathroom to break up whatever domestic situation was occurring behind the closed doors. Isabelle and my mother both exited the restroom. Isabelle hastily making her way to the car with tears running down her red cheeks. My mother, closely following behind her.

It was a quiet ride down to South Bend that evening. Isabelle and my mother did not make eye contact let alone converse with one another. I'm not sure, even to this day, what had happened in that bathroom. Isabelle spent the weekend complaining about her back hurting. Marks appeared on her upper arm where my mother had grabbed her. Red and blue finger imprints slowly appeared throughout the weekend, as well as a bruise that appeared on Isabelle's lower back. The weekend came to a close as the two kept their stalemate in opposition of one another. Not splitting a single word between the two of them all weekend, all the while my mother attempting to produce whatever I requested, without a question. She had spoiled me abnormally more than before that weekend. At the time I suspected it was because she had missed our previous visit while my leg was recovering. Later I came to suspect it was because of what she had done to my sister Isabelle.

The weekend ended as we made our way back to the same McDonald's where the horrific events had begun the Friday before. Our father and Gemma waited in the van outside of the fast-food restaurant. I said my goodbyes to my mother and Jeff as I gathered my belongings; Isabelle hastily leaving the vehicle without the slightest word. Entering the van, we closed the doors when Isabelle could no longer keep her lips sealed.

"How was your weekend?" Our father began.

"I don't ever want to see her again!" Isabelle started, "she hit me! She grabbed my arms and pushed me into the sink in McDonald's all because I wouldn't talk to her!" she frantically yelled as her face turned a flush red.

"What!?" My father turned looking back at Isabelle and me with a horrified gaze.

"We're going to the hospital to have you checked out."

What was supposed to be a good reunion weekend with our mother, turned into another deceitful weekend of neglect. After leaving the hospital, the doctors had confirmed that there were some abrasions and bruises where Isabelle had claimed to be hurt by our mother. Reacting to the previous circumstances, our father was angered. Immediately he filed a petition to revoke visitation rights from our mother. For the next several months, Isabelle and I were mandated to have supervised visitation with our mother until she was deemed safe. Our Grandma Pat and Uncle Fred were the designated supervisors for many visits to come, one Sunday, every two weeks for the next several months.

I had never seen that side of my mother before. I was accustomed to the sporadically emotionally unstable mother, but never had it escalated in a physical manner. At a young age, it became drastically confusing for me. I loved my sister and always wanted to ensure she was safe. However, it took me right back to when we were in the foster home. Once again I failed to protect her. I also loved my mother, or at least I loved the idea of what I wished my mother could be. Hope for the happy relationship I so very much desired became further and further from my grasp. Each opportunity for growth in our mother and child relationship quickly deteriorated with every interaction.

# The Ketchup Sandwich

Things continued array for some time. Only a few short months following, the supervised visits were no longer required. Our mother continued, however, frequently trying to make it up to Isabelle and me. By this time Isabelle had now become a teenager. She was no longer confined to being stuck in the house with her mother on visitation. She made new friends while we visited our mother in South Bend, and was able to find any excuse she could to be out on the town. Times were changing. We eventually grew apart as Isabelle had her new click of friends. These were what I had suspected to be her way of escaping reality. Not just at our mothers, but back home as well.

Eventually, the family dynamics had shifted into groups within the home. Just two years after the birth of Harry, we had added another sibling to the family. Mildred was born. Instead of seven individual children, we were categorized by our house "clicks". We had Mike who was nearing his end of high school, the girls (Isabelle who was now 14 and Marge who was 15), the boys (Chuck and me)both coming into the age of 12, the babies (Harry and Mildred), and the parents. Marge and Isabelle, much like Chuck and me, were close in age. This allowed for each of us to have our own person to play with, or in the girls' case, to "hang with". While the girls grew older, family time dwindled as it served no purpose to a teenage girl. Any thought of wanting to spend the weekends at home with the family became a chore more than a fun thing to do. It was like, totally uncool.

Though Isabelle and I had begun to part ways in areas of interest and our lives, we still maintained the same emotional connection, just as two separate people breaking the co-dependency we once held. She had six other siblings now, and only one that shared her interests. She quickly developed into the shadow of Marge. Marge had a tendency to be a bully to us younger kids and had no desire in spending any more time than she had to with us. Isabelle, unfortunately, began to quickly follow in her footsteps.

Living near the campus of a mental health facility came with quite a few downfalls. On the campus, there was a juvenile facility that housed young men. Mostly teenagers that sadly were close in age to the girls. This in turn led them to frequent their way out of the home and venture off to make new connections with the "troubled boys" in the group home. Just across the street, the two girls would frequently sneak out. After many recurring instances of insubordination, and arriving home late, our parents had enough. My father and Gemma had enough of the girls. Their frequent instances of getting in trouble and hanging out with the wrong crowd, the two eventually landed themselves a grounding. They were not allowed out of the house, nor were they allowed any time on the phone. In a fit of anguish and rage, the two decided they no longer wanted to live under a house of rules.

Marge could no longer take it. Constantly battling

with my father John, she didn't like that her mother would no longer allow her to have her way. To Marge, this new man in her life asserted power. Law and order that she did not wish to adhere to. Tired of the strict house rules she decided it was time to move back to her father's house in Dundee. She wished to move somewhere that didn't care whether or not she was home by nine, let her do as she pleased, and had no formal rules. Within a few weeks, she had made the move.

Isabelle, losing her closest friend Marge, began to take trips where she would stay with Marge for the weekend. It was time for them to regroup and spend time together. Isabelle needed an outlet that fit her lifestyle as a teenager. She too came from the same broken background as myself, and arguably she had it worse than I did. For the many counselors I had to see from the divorce, the kidnapping, the abuse, and the custody battles; being forced into being the product of Munchhausen's she had dealt with more than me. We both desperately desired companionship and acceptance. We each needed our way to venture through the world we so desperately sought to understand. Since our household with my father was a place of rules, the additional escapes became too hard for her to hide. The smoking and drinking and recreational use of pot became all the more difficult to get away with for her.

For weeks this continued until one day we received a knock at the door of the Cutler Mansion. For me, it struck near fear into my already young weary eyes. A woman approached wishing to speak with the children. A woman from the Child Protective Services. One by one each of us were taken into a separate room and questioned. Several hours of inquiries arose on the alleged acts of our home. Discussions of physical abuse, inappropriate touchings, and neglect were brought into question regarding the welfare of our health and nutrition.

"Do you feel safe here?" A voice softly spoke as I sat in the chair at the table across from the woman.

As my eyes focused diligently on my twiddling thumbs resting in my lap "Yes ma'am".

Scribbling on the pad of paper in her lap, she continued to question.

"How about food? Are you eating okay?"

Again, looking to my lap avoiding at all costs eye contact again the hesitant words slipped through my lips. "Yes Ma'am"

"What kind of foods do you eat?" She continued. "Have you found yourself feeling hungry, or that you haven't known where or when you would eat again?

"No ma'am. We eat good"

"One of your siblings mentioned you have been left to eat nothing but mustard and ketchup sandwiches at times. Has this ever happened to you?"

"No ma'am. We eat macaroni or Raman noodles and usually do a family dinner at night time."

Having been placed on the spot, and not knowing how to reply, I could only conjure up a few of the quick and easy meals that came to mind. My mind quickly flooded to a blank. Forgetting about the chicken and mashed potatoes, shepherds' pie, or corned beef hash meals we would also indulge.

"Have you ever been spanked with an object that has left a mark?"

I knew what the woman was seeking for an answer. Yet, I also knew better than to tell the lady what she wanted to hear. Growing up these people were my enemy. Constantly they would tell me how they were there to help, but I knew better. They wanted to destroy my family again. I remember the conversations we had as a family before. These people wanted to take us away. Even years later I could never forget the strange lady that spoke with us after the kidnapping. "Your father is going to get the electric chair and rot in hell!". Those were the only words that ran through my head. These people wanted to take away my happiness.

"No ma'am" I replied.

The interrogation went on for what felt like hours. Finally, she concluded with a thank you as she gathered her things and told me I was free to go play again. Later that evening our family sat and talked about the woman from the Department of Human Services. Almost as if we had to decompress. What were they asking? How did you answer? Fearful if I answered everything right or not, I did not want to be the reason our family was destroyed once again.

The trials seemed nearly endless. The effects had set in from the fallout of the trials. Soon I found myself falling behind in school. Having so much going on in our lives I began hating going to school every day. I couldn't focus on the stuff in class and had a hard time keeping up with the other students. By the time I was 13, we had already attended more than a dozen schools. Charter academies, homeschooling, traditional school, completely different worlds from one another. It was discouraging as we never had time to establish any friends outside of the house and not knowing whether or not I was going to be able to return home became taxing. More frequently I found myself getting into more trouble at school, a few times earning myself a suspension. One time for carving "fuck this" into a school bench while sitting on the sideline to play tennis for gym class.

The custody battles had grown heavier now that the State was brought into the mix. It weighed so greatly, that my sister used this in a surprising act to go live with our mother. We were all caught off guard when she approached my father and Gemma requesting to move in with her mother. My father lowered his head with sadness, but wanting deeply to appease his only daughter, he obliged the request without a fight. He had tried hard to keep Isabelle from following the same path as her mother and Marge, yet, through the stringent rules of the home; Isabelle no longer felt free. He knew she was of age to make the decision from a legal standpoint either way. I was heartbroken. The world kept rapidly changing. Every time we began to settle into a normal routine or think we were finally past the disputes, another would find a way to slip into our lives like a sliver. Finding any escapes became a challenge. We played video games and spent time on the computers for family night. However, it was just a distraction. I hadn't learned really how to cope with everything I had trapped inside my mind.

That was until reading books and writing poetry found a way into my life. I fell in love with a book series my dad introduced to me; Harry Potter. It gave me so much to relate to. Desperately I would disappear into a make-believe world where I too would be called away to a special school where I could find happiness. It became my escape. For a dumb kid who couldn't stay out of trouble at school, and was constantly looked down on for my academic struggles, I had finally found something I could enjoy. I received several of the books by this time. I found two loves that year. Reading those books, and writing poetry after an English teacher introduced me to Robert Frost. Having always been a fan of Dr. Seuss, writing the two together combining the rhyming with emotion; expressing my deepest thoughts became euphoric. It was a good outlet for me. I began to journal a lot those days.

One weekend I went down to my mother's. It was her court-ordered weekend with me. This was going to be a good weekend. We were doing a delayed birthday party for my thirteenth birthday with my "Indiana" family. It was with my mom and her husband's family. It also allowed me to catch up with my sister Isabelle. I looked up to her, and always felt cool when I could hang out with her and her friends because of how much older they were than me. I had received a new Harry Potter book that weekend from one of the brothers of Jeff. I was so excited to have another part of the series I had grown to fall in love with. I unwrapped the book with a smile erupting across my face. I was so happy. Reading had become my drug. It gave me relief to escape to new worlds.

Later that evening we returned to mother's house. I should have known better, but I was too hard-headed to learn. Just as quickly as I could become excited about something, it would just as quickly be taken away. My mother retrieved the book from me. She had recently "rediscovered" God and swore that she was a new person for it.

"Hunny, you can't have this. These books are evil. They are about witchcraft and used to corrupt the minds of children!" She said as she grabbed the book and began walking outside with it.

Confused and heartbroken I followed her out. Jeff, her husband, had just started a fire in the burn barrel outback. Following her, out the door, my heart sank as she pitched it into the fire.

"God wouldn't want this for you."

Frustrated and saddened I ran back to my room in the basement. Grabbing the notebook that I had kept my poetry and journals in; I began to scratch whatever thoughts came to mind. Slashing rapidly as the pencil scraped the paper with a passionate stroke of the lead. Before I knew it I had filled half of my journal. By this time my tears had dried and I placed the journal back under the nightstand where I kept it hidden. Or at least so I thought. The next day I would awake to find it was no longer there. Anxiously I began to shuffle through the nightstand. Bending down and going to my knees I searched frantically for my journal. Throwing my pillows and blankets across the room, tossing anything to the side that didn't resemble a red-covered notebook. After what felt like an hour I conceded defeat. It was gone. I ran up the stairs and confronted my mother.

"Have you seen my red journal? I can't find it anywhere?" I asked shaking and anxious.

"Hunny, we need to talk. I went through your journal last night and I'm worried. We took it to Doctor Hicks this morning to review. He would like to see you this afternoon." She began, forcing a pitied frown across her face.

"Why did you go through my journal!" I exclaimed furiously.

Having already a growing distrust of the world my journal was sacred to me. It contained my deepest fears, my worst angers, and my strongest hurts. It was the one person I could speak with to let my pain and disdain out.

"Well as long as you stay in this house, we can do that. Especially if we feel it is necessary."

"This is bullshit!" I yelled, turning away from her as I stormed back to my room in the basement.

Before I could reach the stairs an angered voice echoed off the wall behind me,

"Do not speak to your mother that way! You had better be ready in one hour for your appointment! Jeff will be back shortly, and we will be taking you to that appointment!" Her voice faded as I continued to my room; slamming the door behind me in a forceful rage.

Just as she had assured me, Jeff came to my door nearly an hour later asking if I was ready to go. Less than thrilled, and feeling defeated, I grabbed my sweater and went up the stairs to his old red Ford.

Only a short drive away we arrived at one of the most belittling and crooked men I would ever meet. Far more menacing than the previous counselors I would have grown to know over the years, Dr. Hicks. We approached the large three-story brick building. Climbing the stairs to the worn-down establishment, eventually arriving at the rugged suite of a washed-up psychologist. We entered the room while Jeff checked us in with the receptionist.

Irritated and repulsed, I waited on the aged, mustard yellow faded seats. Dr. Hicks opened his door and greeted me at his office. I tried not to make eye contact as I took a seat before glancing to his desk to reveal my journals laying open. I had felt betrayed. With my arms crossed and mentally guarded we had proceeded with our impromptu session. As the hour passed of lecturing me on the abnormalities of expressing my emotions; even in a journal, a forced farewell slipped through his crooked lips as he patted me on the shoulder goodbye.

Jeff and my mother were called into his office for a brief discussion before they reappeared to reveal what my issues were. It wasn't that I had journaled my discontent; and despite all of my previous interactions with psychologists and counselors alike, it was that my dad had been manipulating me, according to the doctor. I didn't realize it, but he was the one to declare I had split personalities with burst aggression. Whether it was true or not, that was his designation and what he put in my file.

Much of my distrust of counselors developed by this time. I had already seen over a dozen counselors between the divorce, the kidnapping, my mother's mental health, and my own lack of coping strategies. Even when I wanted to journal how I was feeling, that was used as a weapon against me for a battle I wanted no part of between my parents. I couldn't say I was sad, or angry, or scared. I couldn't express that; I was lonely or afraid. Because of the friendship my mother had with this specific counselor, Dr. Hicks, he twisted it as some mental disorder. Whatever one he could pull from his Diagnostic and Statistical Manual of Mental Disorders, otherwise known as a "DSM", he inserted my emotion into his report as a bi-product of any disorder he thought he could place me in.

I wasn't crazy, or delusional; I was a scared child whose trust was betrayed by too many adults.

We concluded our weekend visit which left me feeling just as disappointed as when I arrived. Upon my return home, I told my dad what had happened. Understanding my sadness, he and Gemma went to the store the following day and purchased the same copy of Harry Potter that had been previously incinerated by my mother. Sharing equal disdain for the events that had transpired; I was scheduled to visit yet another counselor. This one concluded that I was not a deranged child, but rather one who had experienced immense traumas and found a healthy way to journal my emotions. It didn't take long after careful consideration that the court no longer required or mandated me to speak with Dr. Hicks again. After the many counseling visits following they agreed I was not suffering from multiple personalities or burst aggression. Though I had still felt very violated, I didn't let that take away my only friend. I continued to journal and to write. I did become more cognizant of where I left my journals though. Seldom would you find me without it by my side whenever I was at my mothers.

The court proceedings continued for several months as they prodded into our daily lives. Following the many reviews and interviews the State had imposed, they concluded no abuse or neglect had taken place in the home. Considering we were a rather stout family, it did not take long for them to recognize that it would take a lot of ketchup and mustard sandwiches to obtain the weight we each were. It made a pretty solid case that we were not starving. This chapter of my life was just another continuation of the repetitive disruptions I grew to expect. There were always losses incurred after each incident. Unfortunately, this one was the moving of my sister. There was a strange irony of frequenting the continual visits of counselors. They were hired to help, but nearly every one of them seemed to cause more harm than good. My trust quickly deteriorated with adults and the state of our mental health system. If they were the ones hired to protect us, who protects us from them?

# Shackled

Thinking we had finally escaped the nightmare of yet another broken system, we found ourselves moving once again. Trying to regain a new start we moved to Grandville. This was a major turning point in my life; more than likely for the better as I reflect on how it impacted me. We had moved to a more modest home, much smaller than the Cutler Mansion, but it was in a decent neighborhood. It was a four-bedroom home with a small backyard. The area seemed more uppity than we were used to. Then again, going from living next to a mental health hospital to neighbors we could speak with didn't place a hard competition though. We were conditioned by this point to not make new friends. Most of the time we hunkered in our bedrooms playing video games on our computer.

Occasionally Isabelle and Marge stopped to visit. After many years of being away, Marge eventually moved back into the house with us. Her dad and she had a falling out. He began enforcing rules and she no longer cared to stay. Naturally, Chuck and I were paired into the same room. It wasn't an issue, however, by this time Chuck and I really began to separate from one another in hobbies in life. We had continued to share interests in playing video games, however, we were entering our curious age of being teenagers. Girls became an area of interest. I was a short stout kid, and he had developed into a tall blond-haired, blue-eyed, muscular young man. You can imagine which one of us was favored on the "females interested in us" scale.

Life had just started to balance out once again. Though even after the move I found I still didn't fit into school, kids frequently picked on the short, stouter, young me. By this time, I developed a liking for heavy metal music and wearing dark clothes. Occasionally wearing black finger-nail polish and "freak" pants as they were called. There was something enjoyable about feeling like an outcast. Minus the frequents of being bullied. I naturally always felt like an outsider, so the role seemed fitting.

One evening Isabelle came to visit with us. Marge and her boyfriend at the time drove down to pick her up. They came to the house and said their hello's and gave everyone hugs. Shortly after their arrival, they wanted to go to the gas station. Adoring my sister dearly, I tried to tag along. See, secretly I had been smoking for some time. Not the "devil's lettuce", but cigarettes. Marge and Isabelle always helped contribute to my ridiculous habit. They even taught me how to best hide it from our parents. We drove off to get some snacks and drinks. We drove for a short while before pulling up in front of our house once again. This time, however, they did not want to get out of the car. They asked me to take some of the stuff inside and said they would be shortly behind me. Walking up to the door I grabbed the handle before looking back to see the three of them once again drive away. It was only for a short while before the chaos of course erupted. Almost like clockwork.

After hearing the car pull back in front of the house, Marge came in requesting Gemma to meet her and Isabelle outside. Sitting on the couch preparing to play a video game, moments elapsed before Gemma came barging back into the home. Ecstatic and screaming at the top of her lungs; she rushed up the stairs to my father's office.

"EARL! HOW COULD YOU!" She screamed.

Little to our knowledge at the moment Marge and Isabelle claimed our father tried to make an advance on them. The house quickly erupted into immense Hell. Screaming filled the home as my world began to fade black. "Not again," I thought to myself. "I can't take any more of this family!" I felt so overwhelmed. My father gathered his belongings to leave the house. Thinking back to the many things we had been through, I just ran. I had no idea where I wanted to go, I just knew I wanted to be anywhere but home. The screaming in my head became too much. I felt like a rat trapped in a maze. Someone somewhere must have been watching overhead with a note pad and pen. Analyzing our every response. There had to be a reason for all of this. Was I a test subject in some messed up experiment? It was all becoming too routine. No one has this bad of luck. Right?

I ran down the road to a local restaurant. There was a hostess that worked there that I had a crush on. She was older than me by a few years, but I sneaked out occasionally and bummed cigarettes off of her. She was the only safe haven I grew to know in the area.

Not even phased by the cold, snowy weather; I opened the heavy wooden door to the restaurant. Dim mood lights illuminated the stairwell leading down to the basement bar of the restaurant. The woman greeted me as always with that beautiful smile and red lipstick. Just as quickly as she had greeted me, her smile quickly turned to concern as she acknowledged that something was different about today's visit. Something was wrong.

"Hey sweety, what's going on? Why are you crying?" She walked around the podium that she would typically greet the customers at as she sat on the waiting bench with me.

"My family is so...", trying to maintain some sense of composure I sniffle the snot from my nose as I wipe my eyes "fucked up. I'm just tired of it all. Do you have a phone I can borrow? I just need to get out of here".

Knowing from my past that showing emotion could be used against me, and knowing I was lacking in the "attractive male" department; I tried to keep my posture as a strong young man.

"Sure thing dear, you need a smoke?"

"Yes please!" I quickly obliged.

She stood up from the bench as she walked into the back room. I could hear her mutter to her manager, "Hey Paul, I'll be right back, I'm going to step out for a smoke break, can you cover me?"

"Yea, make it quick though". Paul replied, rolling his eyes.

"Thanks, Paul".

She appeared from around the corner as she swung her jacket around her arms and zips it up. Retrieving a phone from her pocket she extends it to me along with a Newport.

"Alright, you ready? I only have a few minutes though.

Do you want to tell me what's going on now?"

I walked around the corner with the smoke perched between my lips, cupping the end as I flicked my lighter, covering the flame from the wind. The sweet smell of menthol and smoke drifted across my nostrils as I take a deep hit, letting the burning sensation fill my lungs. I let a deep sigh out, still trying to compose myself.

"My dad just left my house. My sisters came to visit and said my dad has been making sexual advances to them. All hell broke loose. I just can't take this anymore."

"Are you safe?"

"I don't know anymore." Taking another hit from the cigarette.

"Well, I have to get back in before Pauly yells at me. You want to come to sit when you're done with the phone?"

"Yes please, I'm going to see if I can call my mother to come to get me."

"Anything you need just let me know."

"Thank you".

She takes one last long drag before scrapping the remnants of the cigarette on the side of the wall. Ash and embers from the Newport fall to the ground before she puts it in the ashtray walking back into the building.

Trying to think of something, I resorted to the last person I would want to call for help. Punching the numbers into the phone

I stood outside in the cold as the phone rang. Buzzing on the other end, I sat and waited until finally, a voice answered.

"Hello?" My mother answers.

"Hey mom, it's David."

"Hey, buddy! What's going on?"

Tears began to once again trickle down my face as I slowly erupt into another breakdown. Not knowing how to process everything that had transpired I called the only other person I could.

"Mom I need you to come to get me. I need out of here".

"What's wrong? What happened?"

"I don't want to talk about it right now. I just need to know if you can come to get me." I pleaded.

"Well, Jeff isn't home right now, but maybe we can come to get you in the morning. Where are you at?"

Slipping another drag of my nearly used up cigarette, I let another sigh out exhaling the little bit of smoke left. "I'm at a restaurant a few blocks away. I'm with a friend right now. Can you please just come to get me?" I retort with more urgency and desperation.

"I'll talk to Jeff and see what we can do."

"Alright, I have to hand the phone back now. I'll check back in a little bit."

"Okay, I love you buddy! Why don't we just plan on tomorrow morning?"

"Fine. Love you too. Bye." Frustrated I pressed the red hang-up button. "How the hell can I call my mom crying for help and she just brushed it off? I needed help now, not tomorrow" I thought to myself.

I didn't know what to believe at this point. I knew of my past and the troubles my mother and sisters had continually wrapped our family into, but I also didn't want to disregard them. I was so confused and angry. I just wanted a small taste of a happy family. I wanted to make it a year without fear of losing another person I loved. Having not made any friends, and the constant moves, I was running out of people I cared about. I felt I was in a never-ending war, stuck on the battlefield begging for peace. At this point in my life, I wanted nothing to do with anyone in my family.

With nothing left of my cigarette and nearly frozen tears on my face, I clenched the phone as I slowly trudged back into the building. Walking down the stairs I handed the phone back to my friend with a nod of gratitude before silently taking a seat on the bench. With my head in my hands, I silently wept.

A few hours went by as the bodies shuffled around me. Happy families walking in and out for their family dinners for the weekend. Smiles and laughter echoed through the restaurant. While admiring the lives of those around me, dreaming hopefully one day I too could indulge in a real family; the door once again opens as footsteps clack down the stairs.

"DAVID!" Gemma shouted as she quickly rushed to my side to embrace me in a hug. Mike following closely behind her.

"Oh my God, we have been looking everywhere for you! Are you okay?" She exclaimed wide-eyed and genuine.

"I don't know; I just don't want to go home."

"Well, why don't you come home for now and we will sort this all out, okay? Your father left for tonight, everyone has calmed down. Let's just get through tonight alright?"

"I guess, I don't have anywhere else to go anyways" I snidely remarked, trying once again to keep tears from filling my eyes.

That night felt like the longest I had experienced in a while. We arrived back at the house, but instead of gathering the family in the living room, I decided to retreat to my bedroom. I walked up the stairs and entered the room as Chuck sat, un-phased by the events of the evening at his computer next to his bed. With his headphones on, he didn't even break eye contact from the screen. It was one of the few places I could escape reality for a little while. Reaching to my desk at the foot of my bed I retrieved my headset. Pressing play on my CD player; I placed the headset over my ears as I drowned the noise in my head with the noise of music. Slowly I drifted off to sleep and dreamt of better ventures.

The next morning came just as quickly.

KNOCK KNOCK KNOCK. As the echoes of the thuds radiated through the house Gemma opened the door to see who it was.

"Gemma, where is David?"

Much to Gemma's surprise, Lily stood in the doorway.

"What the hell do you want?" Curling her lip, Gemma crossed her arms to assert a dominant stance.

"I want my son."

"Oh, now you want him? Not any of the times prior he needed you, but now you want him?"

"Look, Gemma, I know what is going on here. Hand him over now, and I will drop any charges or allegations." With a smirk, Lily glared back at Gemma.

"Get the hell off our property, you're not taking him anywhere! John still has custody and you have no right to take him!"

"Fine, we will see you in court then!" Lily replied.

Gemma, clearly upset and frustrated responds,
"FINE!" she yelled slamming the door in Lily's face.

Gemma didn't like to bring me into the mix of the chaos that ensued from my mother. Keeping the previous conversation she had with my mother quiet; Gemma went upstairs to wake me. After a long discussion, she agreed to let me go to my grandmother's where my father was staying. She knew better than anyone, that whenever chaos would come for me, my father was always there to protect me. It was my safe haven. My comfort. I gathered some belongings and packed them in my bag before loading up the car and leaving with Gemma later that evening.

We arrived at my grandmothers' house and once again entered through the creaky swinging door, passing through the aged kitchen and into the living room. This was the same, familiar, smoke-filled house I had recalled spending much of my early childhood in.

I entered the living room to find my father sitting on the couch. He stood up to greet me as he brought me in for a hug. Gemma left to prevent the tension in the home as my father, grandma, uncle Fred, and I sat and watched TV. Fred made us a marvelous dinner as he had been prone to do anytime he had company over. Family or not, he was always sure to offer a great meal.

While sitting on the couch and enjoying our meal, only a few short hours past the time Gemma had dropped me off; we were soon interrupted by reality once again. Fred was in the kitchen cleaning up the dishes following dinner. Several knocks tapped along the glass creaking door. My father and I were in the living room with my grandmother and not aware of the unexpected company. Two detectives in long black jackets entered the living room moments following the knocks.

"Good evening Mr. Kranz" One of them began to say as he reached into his jacket producing a pen and pad of paper. "Do you have a few minutes we can speak with you please?"

"Absolutely. May we step into the other room though?"

"Please, that would be preferred".

"Hey bud, I will be right back. Why don't you stay here with Grandma Pat while we go to talk?" My father rhetorically stated as he stood from the couch looking at me.

"Okay" I responded with a worried and equally confused look on my face.

Though I sat in the other room, my curiosity couldn't help but overtake me. I found myself inching closer and closer to the other end of the couch. A sad attempt to try and eavesdrop drop on the conversation taking place in the other room.

"This isn't the first time this has been brought up officer" I could hear my father explaining. "One of the reasons my kids' mother and I divorced was because she had tried a stunt like this before. That's why I have custody of the children now. After I remarried, Gemma's children didn't like me. After I began to cut down on the rules the girls wanted out of the house and both went to go live with their other parent."

"Would you be willing to come down and take a polygraph?"

"Definitely. When should I do that? I have my son tonight, but I can come down anytime tomorrow or after."

"David!" My grandma whispered at me. She could tell

I was being nosy. I quickly diverted my attention from the dining room and scooted back to my proper place on the other side of the couch.

Nearly an hour passed when the detectives left the house. My father reappeared into the living room with a calm smile as he sat next to me. "Hey bud, don't worry. They are just doing their job. I don't want you to worry about any of this. You have school tomorrow, why don't you get some sleep and I will take you to school tomorrow."

Nodding in compliance, I went to bed. Uncertain of what would come next I was at least content knowing that I was with my father right now.

The months seemed to drag. The court cases continued as questions of physical and sexual abuse came into question. The State had no desire of pursuing criminal charges as each allegation came back unprecedented. No criminal charges arose from the allegations made. The Department of Human Services, on the other hand, had no intentions of letting a perfectly good opportunity to disrupt a family go to waste. Within only a few short weeks they determined we had been neglected and abused according to state law. Being paddled with a cutting board was abuse.

It didn't take long for all of us children to be removed by the state. Not physically, but legally. We were officially wards of the state. Though we were able to reside in the house with Gemma, my father was not allowed to return home, and the state was legally our guardian. Another batch of counselors were assigned to us children, and a caseworker was delegated to determine what was best for us children.

By this time, I could no longer cope well in a regular

school system. By thirteen years old I attempted to run away again. I couldn't seem to fit in with the other kids in school. I couldn't focus on my classes and had the attention span of a child in a room full of toys. Nothing interested me anymore. Not even the once treasured journaling and poetry. How could I read and write such beautiful words in a world so ugly. All I wanted to do was play video games to escape my realities.

After only a few months at school, I tried to run away. It was near lunchtime and there was enough movement through-out the hallways that I managed to slip out of one of the side doors. I began walking down the road before a staff member who saw me sneak out stopped me. Within the hour they had me and Gemma in the office to discuss my leaving.

It took less than a day for them to determine I was no longer a good fit in a traditional school system. This was one of the most pertinent changes in my direction in life. I was terrified at first and didn't know what to expect. Another school change was set in motion. This time to Orion Alternative Junior and Senior High School. I didn't know much of what to expect, however, the reputation of them was that they were for troubled kids. It's where the dumb and bad kids went, I believed initially. Was I dumb? Was I a bad kid? I didn't know what to believe anymore. I just knew I certainly wasn't normal. Stuff like my family didn't happen to normal people.

A week went by before starting my new endeavors. My first day rapidly approached as I was dropped off at the new school. We arrived at a much smaller building than I was used to. The tall white building resembled more of a church than a school. Two glass doors led into the entrance opening to a large common area with round tables and chairs. The school had only one hallway, and couldn't have had more than forty students in total. I entered the office on my left as I awkwardly waited in the chair against the wall.

"Hello, you must be our new student?" The soft voice of the office lady warmly asked.

"Yes, Ma'am. My name is David. I don't know what classroom I am supposed to go to?" I replied as I timidly approached the counter.

"No problem dear. Welcome to our school. It looks like you will be in Chip's class. That is straight back and to the left." She politely advised me. Handing me a piece of paper of my new schedule.

I hadn't had just one classroom in years. It was rather odd. Folding the paper she had given me; I placed it in my pocket as I left the office. Students all lounged in the common area waiting for classes to begin. I left the office as the overwhelming presence of judging stares engulfed any sense of comfort I may have had left. Quickly making my way to the classroom, I had no desire to try and socialize. I didn't know these kids, and I was certainly nobody worth wanting to know. Having been traditionally picked on in school, I was not ready to start this new adventure making a target of myself once again. It was rather odd being one of perhaps twelve middle-schooler students in a high school. Especially one of this size.

Just as quickly as the anxiety and discomfort had set in, it just as quickly went as I was greeted by the staff members and approaching students. I entered the classroom and identified the first open chair I could find. I dropped the bag to my side taking my seat. As I tried to lower my head, embedding myself into my own little world, I was pulled out by two boys and a cute girl approaching the table I was at. Expecting to be picked on for being the new kid, I was taken aback by the inquisitive questions as they asked what school I came from. Just as an inmate moving to a new jail, where we came from and why we were there tied into the bonds. It was relieving.

Within a few short weeks at the new school, I learned that everyone here was an outcast. Just like me, all of them came from some sort of a broken home. There was a sense of camaraderie with each of us. Even the ones that had no desire to associate with us at least had a similar expectation that none of us were accepted by the regular world. I adapted well to the new environment.

The teachers worked astoundingly with all of us students. Our English teacher was a prime example. He always cared about our well-being and remained vigilantly thoughtful to the success of the students. He always had a way of understanding the struggles each of the students were going through, Bob Genetski, or as we would call him, E-Bob. We had two Bob's at the school, one that taught English, and one that taught math. It was uniquely different that we didn't have to refer to any of our teachers as a Mr or Mrs. Just as they called us by first name, we too would call them by first name. There was always something about that which encouraged, and made me comfortable, that we were equals in humanity. It created a good interpersonal bond for each of the students.

Coming from such a broken history and the constant

seeking of acceptance, I rapidly found myself excited for school once again. My grades quickly climbed, and I was able to say for the first time in a while that I had friends. People I was excited to socialize with when I arrived at seven-thirty in the morning every morning. I was barely thirteen when I had started at the school. Though it probably wasn't the best place for my physical health, it was drastically better for my mental health. Encouraging my parents to drop me off earlier and earlier each day, I met with my friends just before the start of school and would sneak down the road around the corner with them to get our morning nicotine in. Having been introduced to smoking only a few years earlier, I was in a crowd that had access, and willingness to share with a young kid like myself.

As my bonds with the new school grew, my relationship with Chuck slowly dwindled. He didn't want to be involved in the chaos of the home any more than I did, yet, he also was attending a different school. Just as Isabelle and I had once upon a time began fulfilling our own identities, Chuck and I began to grow distant also. All of the cliques that were once had in the home quickly deteriorated. Any process of unison in the home was now gone.

The court cases continued, occasionally removing me from school. Those were the harder days to deal with. I was bounced frequently between going to see my father and stay a few days a week at my grandmothers' with him, staying home with Gemma, going to visit my mother, and attend school. Spending hours outside of a courtroom waiting to meet with my guardian ad-litem was the last place I wanted to be. My father, knowing of my struggles, had lined up a mentor for me while I waited. His good friend, Paul, attended the hearings with us and sat outside of the courtroom with me to teach me a new magic trick. We arrived at the courthouse early in the morning and sat on the hardened wooden-bench with a deck of cards. Each hearing I would learn a new trick or skill that he encouraged me to work on over the next few weeks before the next hearing. By fourteen I became a master with a deck of cards. One-handed shuffling, cutting the deck with one hand, and performing flourishing and artistic maneuvers, manipulating them to do whatever I desired. It was one of the few things I had control of those days. It became my new escape. The best part was, as much as I enjoyed performing this feat of sleight of hand, it equally brought joy and curiosity to those I would grow to perform for. That year had many growing and life-altering benefits for me. I had fallen in love with my school, fallen in love with magic, started my own magic business, and finally found a mental escape from the chaos. I was doing well enough in school that I was able to advance into the ninth grade halfway through the year since I was performing exceedingly well in all of my classes. It was no longer a challenge. As one should have it though, not all good things last.

In 2003 we finished our school year just like any other. Excited to have a safe haven to return to, I quickly found that to not be the case for the following school year. We were moving, once again. This time, nowhere near anything familiar. We were moving to Allegan. A small town right in the asshole of Michigan.

Yet, as concerned as I was initially on the move, I quickly learned to embrace it as I was now be attending a new Alternative High School. Timid and worried at first; I found it to be a continuing comfort and contributor to my growth as a successful human being; it was Allegan Alternative High School. Just as I had previously encountered upon my arrival to Orion, I once again arrived to a small school with one hallway. The exception, however, was this one had a gym instead of a common area.

Arriving at the school I quickly drew the attention of the students. As a green-haired, metal music listening, clad bracelet magician; I quickly found myself able to fit in. Just as the previous, we were a close family of outcasts in the single hall of the alternative education system.

One afternoon following my walk home from school on a cold winter afternoon, I would walk through the peaceful graveyard. A path I had learned to be the most direct and quiet route home. I and a newfound friend were walking when a shaggy-haired, and rather goofy kid approached us, asking if he could walk home with us. Without skipping a beat, he integrated himself alongside us as if we had been friends our entire lives.

"Hey, what's up man?" He began, "Do you mind if I walk with you guys?"

"Not at all, I'm Kranz. What's your name?" Adjusting the straps on my backpack trying not to trip over my flared-out baggy Tripp pants.

"I'm Levi. You just started at the alternative didn't you?" Levi asked while he pulled out a pack of Marlboro Reds. He forcefully tapped the pack against his hand to pack them.

"I did. We just moved here a few months ago from Grand Rapids. I hate to be a bum, but can I steal a smoke from you?" I asked.

Unwrapping the clear plastic from the pack he extended two cigarettes out, spacing them to indicate he would oblige the request.

"Here man, no problem." Handing me the cigarette he shuffles through his army green jacket to find a lighter.

"Man winter sucks!" He began as his shivering fingers cupped the end of the cigarette clicking the lighter with the other.

"Indeed! I think I'm going to surround my house with space heaters so it can just be summer all year round!" I chuckled as he handed me his lighter.

From that day forward, Levi and I became best of friends. He lived just a few miles down the road from me and was only a month younger than I was. His father was the vice president of a local motorcycle club. Both of us sharing similar interests in computer gaming, and his fascination with magic we hit it off instantly. He came to be the closest thing to a brother I would find. By the end of that year, I found myself hanging out with him nearly daily.

Whether it was the trial by fire that I became more readily able to bounce back from the changes, or the fact that the trials of the court proceedings were coming to an end; I began to feel confident and comfortable. That year was the start to the most stability I had in a long time.

# Burn It Down

After the previous year's chaos and things returning to normal, I grew accustomed to always wondering when the next shoe would drop. I was a skeptic of everything. Yet, my father returned home finally. The court cases, that had been drawn out for nearly three years, were thankfully coming to a close. After the disparaging and gruesome hoops we jumped through, and the constant threat of being removed from the home by the state; it was finally over. After many psychological evaluations, it was determined my step-sister was prone to create allegations for the stimulation of the drama. That, combined with the lead case-worker admitting on the stand that she fabricated evidence and lied to the courts; was enough for them to dismiss all charges. The court ordered that my father and Gemma be re-instated with full guardianship of the children and my father could return home. It was determined the allegations were unfounded and the separation of our father being out of the home was more detrimental to our well-being for developmental growth.

At no fault to Gemma, she was forced to be a single mother for those three years. Between working to support us, battling the court cases, fear of the children being removed any day; she did the best she could. Unfortunately, it left us fending for ourselves at times. Harry and Mildred were fairly young at this time and had little understanding of the events that were going on. The downside, much like young David, was they had now been exposed to the system of counselors and lawyers that plagued me at such a fragile age. Even to a young mind, it has long-lasting effects. Having been eerily reminded of the many years ago of what could happen much like Isabelle and I had experienced; I wanted to maintain my own identity, but also felt a responsibility to protect them. With the absence of a protector in the home, I became the support to try and hold the family together. At times feeling much like I was playing tug-of-war with me at the center of the world, as each effort was pulling my arms to opposite ends of the earth.

I had grown to seek approval outside of the home. This grew a closer bond and dependency on my friends around me. Their families began accepting me as their family. Though my father was able to return home, much had changed. Even with me visiting him normally; the lack of consistency in the daily life of a growing boy made it difficult to navigate life. I had felt like I was being forced to grow up long before I was ready. His return offered relief.

After my fathers' return home, my father and Gemma began working on a non-profit medical clinic. Diving deep into the ministries of the recently reunited family; with my father's background in business and Gemma's in nursing, it became a passion. They had envisioned it to be to help those who didn't have insurance to be able to have free health care. For the next several months they would devote their time to family and the clinic. By this time I was doing well myself with a new vision of hope. I was seventeen years old and had become known in the local school system. I was the green-haired kid that dressed...different. Though the green hair only lasted a few short years, it was enough to draw a connection to who I was for the kids I attended school with, and the friends I gained in the new town. I even managed to secure a job at the local Village Market as a bag boy. Things were finally looking up.

After watching the clock count down, the school day had ended. The halls flooded with students as we all filed out the front doors to freedom. Kids each retreating to their vehicles while others slowly trudged down the road to the small empty park that consisted of a run-down tennis court and a picnic table. A few friends and I, as our daily tradition would have, wandered down to the desolate park at the end of the road to have our after school cigarette. The police frequented by here, but as long as we weren't causing any trouble they mostly left us alone. A few kids here and there found themselves embarking on a new minor in possession charge if the officer was feeling extra rambunctious that day, however, for the most part, they left us be.

As the few cars pulled up next to the park and we chatted about party plans for the evening and whatever assignments we had that day we each sparked up our cigarettes while our notorious beggar from class would go person to person looking for a spare smoke to bum. I sat and took a drag from the cigarette as the invigorating smoke filled my lungs. The morbid joy as I inhaled and let out a slight sigh of relief as the smoke trailed off of my lips.

As juniors and seniors, we were required to take a

vocational skills trade in order to graduate. Johnier that year I tried my hand at electrical mechanical skills. Come to find out, I did not have those skills. Shortly into the program, I decided to switch to a graphic design class to keep me occupied. I wasn't very artistic, but through my masterful coping skills of computer gaming, I could find my way around the computer program. I actually found I was better than I thought at it; better than my electrical skills at least. We had a big competition coming up in a week. As one of our projects, we had been asked to write a speech for competitive purposes to give in front of an audience on a topic of the school's choice. Skills USA is what it was called. It was for students to speak on the topic of success and resilience. Having a brief background in resilience, I was able to make it to the semi-finals for the state competition. We were preparing to go to Lansing to give an award-winning speech to hopefully gain an opportunity to go to the nationals.

This was a major opportunity, especially for alternative students like myself. We wanted to show the world that we weren't just some adolescent misfits who couldn't cut it in the real world. Having already won first place in locals and regionals; this was my opportunity to place Allegan Alternative High School on the map. I had spent the last three weeks preparing my best speech and finding the best suit I could to land a shot at even placing.

We stood around laughing and joking talking about each of our competitions as sirens could be heard in the distance.

"Someone's having a bad day." I chuckled, amused by my remark.

Little did I know that karma had a slick response to even something as subtle as that comment. Smoke could be seen in the distance as the grayish-black trail emitted towards the sky. We each filed into our cars and made our way home. I pulled out onto the main stretch of road and drove across the bridge listening to music. The smoke grew closer and closer as I approached my street. I looked to see where the trail had stemmed from, I began growing more and more concerned as to the cause of the sight. I turned down my road, just bridging the slight hill that would peak right near the base of where my empty driveway should be. However, today my driveway was not empty. Fire trucks filled the streets as cars lined the road behind them as onlookers stood on the sidewalks and near their cars looking to where our house stood. My father stood outside in an oversized shirt and shorts that the neighbor had lent him, a bandage encasing his arm. My little sister and brother stood close by. Uniformed men in turn-out gear walked in and out of our once complete house as smoke and ash filled what used to be where our windows were placed.

I was stunned. Just eight hours earlier I had walked out of a finished home. When I returned, I found out that we were the ones that were going to have that bad day. A man in a white helmet approached my father advising him that it was safe for our family to enter the home to gather some belongings, however, we would not be able to return to our house.

"We have contacted the Red Cross, they should be here shortly with some supplies and information to get you a hotel for a while." The fire chief began. "I am very sorry for your loss, the Red Cross should be able to help you and your family navigate through this tough time. There is significant damage to the kitchen and living room, but we were able to save the rest of the home."

"Thank you so much!" My father humbly replied. "It sucks, but at least we can rebuild".

Trying to grasp what was happening a car pulled up behind ours as a curly-haired mullet emerged from the driver's door. It was one of my teachers, one of my mentors, and a friend; Mark.

"Hey, David! Are you guys ok?!" He questioned.

"I'm not quite sure yet. I guess everyone is safe, but our home is destroyed. We don't know where we are going to stay yet." I replied.

"It will be okay, we will do whatever we can to try and help you out. I will let the staff know." He responded genuinely concerned.

"Thank you," I mumbled still trying to comprehend what had just unfolded.

My father approached to offer his thanks to Mark for his concern. He handed me a trash bag a neighbor had given him and told me to go grab a few things to bring with for now, if it were at all salvageable. I grabbed the black trash bag from his hand and approached the dark doorway. A musty smoke smell was strongly emitted throughout the home. As I entered the house, it was dark and damp. The once white walls were now stained with smoke and bubbled paint. The fan from the ceiling had melted plastic weeping down as the light bulbs were disfigured. The furniture was destroyed with water and insulation decorating the floor. It was as if I had just entered a war zone. With hints of familiarity, the rest of the home was almost unrecognizable.

Trying to watch where I stepped, trudging through the debris, I made my way to the back of the house to our stairwell that led up to my room. The smell of smoke was inescapable, however, the smoke stains slowly began to dissipate from the walls as I entered my room. Thankfully, our door had been closed that morning. It helped keep most of our room protected, however, the smoke had no restraint. One by one I began to fill the bag with any clothes I could find that weren't ruined. Picking up pictures and items, not knowing what would remain once we returned. The speech I had spent weeks on was destroyed, and that perfect suit, lay covered in water and soot. I sat on my bed and lowered my head. Trying to comprehend everything that had just happened, stuck in a daze. The bag resting on the floor to my side. "How do you pick up your entire life and fit it into one bag?" I wondered to myself. Today was the day we became homeless.

Following the events, we would find that my younger sister, Mildred, had decided to go into the kitchen to attempt to cook some food. Unknowingly to my father who was home with Harry and Mildred at the time, Mildred went into the kitchen where some oil sat in a pan. She had helped Gemma cook meals in the past and was trying to learn to help out more with the meals in the home. Having learned about having to boil water, she applied the same logic to the pan of oil. She had turned the stove on and let it sit, patiently waiting for it to boil to drop in the food. To her surprise, as the oil began to boil and pop, it would rapidly grow out of control as the hot oil quickly erupted into an inferno. Reaching to the cupboards, and quickly spreading to the ceiling, the room filled with heavy black smoke. In a panic, she ran to the living room to get my father who was working at his computer. As the kitchen door swung open and the frantic seven-year-old girl ran out, my father saw the heavy smoke trailing close behind her. Gathering the children and the phone they hastily made their escape and called the fire department.

Later that evening Red Cross made contact with my father and they put us up in a local hotel. Two weeks was all they could afford us. Gift cards to restaurants accompanied the hotel stay while we tried to figure out our next steps. Trying to make the best of the events that had unfolded before us, our parents had bought a take-out dinner and we decided to just have an evening of pizza and movies. We needed something to take our minds away from reality. I, on the other hand, could not be removed from the reality at hand. Between the speech, school, and wrapping up my last two years of high school, I didn't want to move. I didn't want to have to leave it all behind. With everything we had been through growing up, I had finally found a place I felt established and welcomed. This was, in essence, my home.

The day finally arrived where I would have to load a bus at school to head to Lansing for our much-awaited state competition. Feeling like I had just lived off rations and dirty clothes, I gathered what would be the cleanest outfits and prepared for my temporary escape. Even though my speech had been destroyed and my suit ruined, the show must go on. I packed my bags that morning and said goodbye's to my father and Gemma. I hugged them as

I prepared to head out the door knowing I would not be returning for a few days. My father, as he approached to hug me stretched out his arm. "Here, I know it isn't much, but Gemma and I want you to be able to get some food and have a couple of spending dollars while you're gone. Try not to let what happened to us ruin this experience for you. Good luck bud, you will do great!" He said placing a hand on my shoulder as he gave a calming smile.

"Thanks, Dad, I appreciate it," I replied with a warmed smile.

Picking up my bags I said one last goodbye as I walked out the door. That morning as I boarded the bus it was hard to push through the emotions. Trying deeply to put the house fire out of my mind, with the constant "sorry's" of teachers and fellow students, it became more and more difficult to push it aside. We each found a seat and rested our bags beneath the seats. Most of the other kids had grabbed a pillow or sweater to find a way to catch a rest on the trip, while other students sat to the back of the bus filling it with echoing chatter. I watched as everyone around me continued their day. To them, it was just another day. For me, it was an irony. In less than twenty-four hours I would be giving a speech on resilience and champions at work. Overcoming hardships in life. Funny how life throws that at you now and then. While the other students rested or chatted, I spent this time reflecting. Trying to grasp what I could throw together last minute as a speech. Trying ever vigilantly to recall the words previously transpired on the now ash ridden speech I had previously prepared.

Before I knew it, the bus came to a halt. We had arrived. What had felt like the only moment in my mind had been hours in the real world. Letting out a sigh, I knew I was no closer to the beginning, let alone concluding my supposed, state winning speech. Grabbing our bags, we all filed off of the bus and made our way to the hotel. The excitement and adventure-filled the eyes of the other students. Looking around I noticed Goodwill not more than a half-mile walk from the hotel. Cutting through a few fields would make it only a short distance walk.

"Alright everyone, before you go anywhere you need to check into your rooms and in with your teachers. After that you can request to sign out for free time" Mr. Shank loudly spoke as the students exited the bus.

Hurrying to get to my room, I may just have enough time to pick up a last-minute suit. Piling into the hotel we each dispersed in groups to our rooms. Quickly I would make my way ahead of the pack to get to my room, assignments were called out as I and two other students would share a hotel room. This was our assigned group for the weekend. Anything we wanted to do, we had to make sure we had our group with us.

"Great" I wondered to myself, "How am I going to convince them to go to the store with me?"

"Man, I really need to get some food!" Carlos exclaimed.

"I saw a Ce Ce's Pizza across the lot!" John said excitedly.

I reached my hand into my jeans, reaffirming the loose twenty-dollar bill that sat lonely in my pocket. Knowing this had to last me the entire weekend, I figured I could probably scrape by with a few dollars and the infamous McDonald's dollar menus.

"I'm not really hungry" I began as my belly secretly ached in hunger. "I'll still go with you guys though. Would you mind if we stopped at the Goodwill first?" I gently requested.

"Sure." They both said in agreement.

As we walked into the Goodwill I stood at the entrance like a lost puppy looking for its owner. Glancing around the large store a clerk approached. "Is there anything we can help you boys find?" She offered in an assisting tone.

"Where are your dress suits, ma'am?" I timidly asked.

"Right back here." She replied with a smile.

We approached a wall lined with presumably used outfits. White dress shirts and pants with assortments of ties and old shoes cluttered the back of the store. Looking for several moments I found my size in a white dress shirt with some moderately compatible dress slacks. Thinking back to what my dad had told me about the importance of color when matching ties, I reached for the red tie hanging temptingly from the rack. Knowing that red was a color of power and confidence I felt it was fitting in building my confidence. I needed much of both under the current circumstances. I grabbed some size eight leather dress shoes that sat about the table to my side. My size was waiting readily for me on the display table. Looking carefully at each of the tags, I felt like Sherlock Holmes, investigating the best deal to stretch my limited funds. Approaching the counter nervously, hoping my failed math attempts might serve me in better light this time, I placed my items on the roller. One by one the clerk scanned each item while attempting small talk. Nodding aimlessly with a forced grit smile I watched the digital display like a hawk, hoping the total would not breach my allotted funds. With so much on the line, and making it this far, would twenty dollars be the final breaking point for me?

"$21.64 dear!" She politely requested.

Taxes...I forgot about the taxes. My head began to sweat as a line of people waiting behind me in the line appeared growingly impatient. Knowing I did not have that much, I nervously opened my wallet to reach for my lonely twenty. While opening my wallet my ID card from Kalamazoo Community College flashed in the direction of the clerk.

Catching the clerk's eye, she asked, "Oh, are you a student?"

"Yes ma'am," I exclaimed, not giving an opportunity to explain that I was just a part-time for a trial program at the school. We attended a one day a week professional development class to try and earn some college credit before graduation.

"Oh, well let me fix this for you then! We offer a 15 percent student discount!" She remarked.

Letting out a sigh as the patrons behind me rolled their eyes impatiently. What was an inconvenience for them ended up being a blessing for me.

"That will be $18.39 then dear." She said looking back at me.

I grab the twenty from my wallet and hand it to the clerk with overwhelming relief. Not only was I able to obtain the suit for my speech, I even had enough left over to buy a burger from McDonald's. Thank God for the dollar menu. I grabbed my bag from the counter and walked out the door. Ready to fulfill my promise to my group we left for their much-awaited pizza buffet.

Returning to the hotel I was left with one more step. Preparation for the speech. As the night drew longer I began to recall bits and pieces of the speech. Trying to piece together each memory of a sentence, I tried placing pen to paper to re-create my speech. One o'clock quickly approached. Knowing we had to be up in a short six hours I couldn't push through any longer. I wasn't sure what I was going to do, but I knew I needed to sleep to have any coherent thought the next morning. Seven AM rapidly approached. Feeling tired still, I stepped into the bathroom for my morning shower and slipped on my $18.39 suit. This was it. Game time.

Students flooded the hallways as we left our rooms. Each of us making it to our respective locations. Mine, however, was the banquet hall of the hotel. I was the only student remaining from our prepared speech category. Standing nervously outside of the large wooden double doors anxiously waiting to hear my name called. Minutes felt like hours until finally, the loud creaking of the double doors echoed through the hall. Another young contestant exited the door as a man in a suit held the door.

"David Kranz" He called out inquisitively.

"That's me, sir!" I said as I took a deep breath prior to entering the room.

I walked through the double doors as it opened to a large room with a table and three chairs sitting at the center. A small portable stage with a podium stood in front of the three judges. I quickly learned that a once prepared speech was about to turn into an extemporaneous one. Puffing my chest out slightly and raising my shoulders to lift my head, I approached my position in front of the three judges. Standing before them I took one last deep breath.

"Hello, my name is David Kranz." I began, "Ironically,

I stand before you now to speak in regards to champions at work. Champions at work to me reflects on one's ability to display resilience. Today I offer a personal example of what that looks like to me. Less than a week ago our house had burned down. Standing before you today I offer the sincerest form of that resilience. Not twelve hours ago I arrived in this city with twenty dollars to my name. My suit, my prepared speech, and my pride had all been tragically burned when our house caught fire. When I arrived, I quickly sought a local Goodwill where I would use my twenty dollars to purchase the suit you see standing before you today. All that I had was engulfed in flames, yet, here I stand discussing what champions at work means to me. It is those, who even in the face of adversity, aspire to overcome those obstacles to create a better life." I continued.

Trying to create my speech as I went, I found myself quickly nearing its end. I offered my thanks to the judges before nervously exiting the stage and retreating back to my room. Hours had passed as many other students, just like myself, anxiously waited outside of the large banquet room. One by one they each entered the room and left looking more like a ghost than when they entered. Finally, the day was nearing its end. The announcements for the winners would be announced shortly after dinner.

Sitting on my bed trying to disengage from the world around me, I disappeared into the world of television. The sounds of video games and laughter echoed through the hallways of the hotel floor as students arrived back to their rooms waiting, just like myself, to find the results. After many grueling hours, a knock would percuss off of our door.

Knock, knock, knock, "They are ready to announce the winners. We need everyone downstairs for the ceremony." Mr. Shank announced.

Students hastily gathered their shoes and jackets and filed out of the rooms like cattle. Each making their way to the large community room that housed everyone attending the event. Each of us searched for a vacant seat and wait for the results to be announced. The lights dimmed as the speaker approached the front of the room. Projectors placed on the walls to be displayed for the back rows to see and hear. One by one the announcements were called off for each of the competitive categories. I sat watching the screens waiting until finally, I clenched the chair in front of me in anticipation as I heard them say, "Now for the prepared speech competition". I wanted to hear the results but equally was nervous. "Our Winner is" as the name echoed through the room on the loudspeaker all of the voices around me began to fade as my hopes quickly drained from my body. It wasn't me. Trying not to cry, knowing I had given it my all, I still could not help but feel disappointed. The rest of the evening fell to the wayside as they concluded their announcements. Offering their congratulations to each candidate that participated they instructed the students to return to their rooms for our final stay before heading back to our respective towns.

It wasn't that I lost that hurt. It was that I knew I could have done better. I wanted so badly to be successful for all of the teachers that had done so much for me. It was our opportunity to put Allegan Alternative High School on the map. It was our opportunity to show the world that alternative school students were a lot more than just troubled children. We were normal kids who had experienced abnormal circumstances in life. That despite what people believed, we were fighters. Every step of the way, every encounter, we gave it our all when we were told we couldn't do anything. I had let them down.

After returning home, my father and Gemma informed me they had found a temporary house for us. The church we attended had a vacant house next to the church they used for meeting and storage, but they were willing to put our family up for a short time while we rebuilt our home. The only problem was, it was nearly twenty miles away and I didn't have a car. I couldn't move again. I didn't want to leave everything I was comfortable with. I had endured so much instability in my life. Even though moving was familiar to me, I didn't want to anymore. This was where I parted ways with my family. I pandered to my friends, much without any hesitation from them offering a couch for me to sleep on. For weeks I bounced around staying at a different house every couple of days. That was until a friend said that enough was enough.

"I talked to my mom. You can't keep bouncing around from house to house man. We agreed you can just stay with us. We already got a bed for you." Travis exclaimed. I could see the pity in his eyes, I hated the feeling of pity, but respected and appreciated the love that came with it. For the next year, I lived with him.

I owed a lot to Travis and his mother. He lived in a two-bedroom hud home. I remember entering the house that first night. Walking through the door and passing through the laundry room as it entered a clean kitchen and dining area. Walking across the reflective laminate flooring of the kitchen a small black dog would happily greet us. Baby girl was her name. She loved company, especially if they offered a friendly pat on their way past her. To the other side of the home was Travis' room. Travis and I shared his room. On his floor was a mattress that I would sleep on with my bag of clothes resting in the corner near his computer desk. We became even closer friends while I stayed there. With the help of his mother and him, I learned how to become a self-sufficient man. Though they didn't charge me to stay with them, she did expect me to take well care of myself. I didn't know how to do laundry or really fold clothes. That was one of many living habits she was quick to rectify.

I had begun to learn to pull my weight around the home. From doing dishes, tending to my own laundry, and cooking my own meals at times. It was a small price to pay for the gratitude that was extended.

Summer rapidly approached. This was exciting because it meant we could finally begin the rebuilding of our home. Every day I went to work at the small grocery store down the road from Travis' house. When I got out of work, I started going down to the burned house. Frequently I found comfort in being able to help rebuild. Something was satisfying in watching something that was once beautiful, that had been destroyed in a fiery inferno, being rebuilt to something beautiful again. Day by day, nail by nail, rubble by rubble, the house began to come together once again. After a long year, we were able to return home.

Though I had still frequented visits with my family, I had become comfortable in my new life. Nearly absent from strife, while rebuilding the house I found I would also be rebuilding myself. I no longer had to feel like the mediator or care-taker of the home for that short while. I was able to experience all of the gratifications of life that I had been deprived of for so long.

By the time the house was completed, I had finished my last year of high school. Chuck had shipped out for the Marine Corps while I was searching for my passion in life. I had already been attending college since the start of my senior year of high school, so the transition from one to the other was easy. Having spent a year transitioning from different houses, the concept of independence was no longer foreign to me. The only difference this time was, having purposely put off dating anyone for so long, I was missing an important aspect of companionship. I had tried dating a few times during my last few years of high school, but I always felt like an outcast. I was the kid that would bounce around and managed to fit into every group. Everyone came to me for advice, but I was not really the cool kid-type either. I was too "square" for the girls that attended school with me. Being at the alternative a lot of the girls liked to party, drink, smoke, and some even had kids by their senior year. None of that caught my attention as appealing. The downside was, it meant I would be emotionally lonely when it came to a different type of comfort. A small price to pay I guess. My father would always tell me to focus on school before humoring the nonsense of dating.

During my first year of college, I had become a little braver about the idea of dating again. I would meet girls, however, none of it developed into anything more than a casual hangout. Something always felt like it was missing. That was until one day I would be struck completely off-guard.

One of my friends and I had been driving around aimlessly. Cory was his name. We had just installed a new stereo system into his car and were making our way to a local super-market to kill some time. We stopped at a local gas station that we frequented. There was only one that was open on our side of town for that time of night. We both walked in to purchase our standard energy drink and pack of Marlboro Reds. In a small town such as Allegan, there wasn't much to do anyway really than drive and smoke. This time, however, someone was standing by the counter next to our regular tenant. A gorgeous, brown-haired beauty stood at the counter next to the lottery tickets talking with the clerk. I wanted to make eye-contact so bad, yet at the same time was too shy to try. She had a smile that took my breath away. I was hooked. Cory and I grabbed our things and left back out to the car to pump the gas.

"Man, that chick in there is gorgeous!" I told Cory, looking back to the counter through the window.

"So, go talk to her then." He chuckled as he unscrewed the fuel cap.

"Man, I don't know. I don't even know what I would say to her."

Removing the handle from the gas pump and placing it into the car he looked back at me,

"Look, if you don't go talk to her then I'll go talk to her for you. Fuck it" He said challengingly.

Attempting to call his bluff, I had chuckled in response and began to get back into the car. Underestimating his sincerity; he hung up the nozzle and began walking back into the store. As quickly as I buckled my seat belt I pulled it back off, hastily exiting the vehicle and attempting to catch up to him without looking like a creeper.

"Did you boys forget something?" The clerk said with a smile splitting across her face.

Leaning on the counter near the register he replied "You see, my friend here is a pussy and was too afraid to ask. But, he was wondering if your friend here would like to go hang out with us?"

My face began to turn red, I shouldn't have called his bluff I was thinking. Secretly deep down though, I knew I wouldn't have been able to ask. Just as I was nervous, I would soon be equally grateful.

"Where are you guys going?" The girl answered with a slight chuckle as a beautiful smile crept across her face.

"We're just going to the store" I began, inserting myself into the conversation to try and regain some sense of redemption of my shy quality. "We just put some subs in the car and are just hanging out."

The clerk and the girl looked at one another giggling. The clerk looked to Cory and me, we had known the clerk for some time as we frequented this station.

"Now boys, this is my niece Jessica, she would love to go with, but you better be good to her!" She stated.

Jessica looked at her aunt and then back to us. "Yes, I will go with" She smiled.

I was shocked, I had never been good with anything like this. I always had low self-esteem myself, and to my surprise, the girl I would fall in love with at first sight would say yes. Standing there with her straightened long brown hair, glowing with her perfectly white reflective smile in her black sweater covering her tank top, I didn't want my eyes to stray. This had to be too good to be true. Much to my surprise, it was not; God had given me something gorgeous in an otherwise ugly world. Cory knew what he was doing, he had just single-handedly helped organize what I would learn to be mine and Jessica's first unofficial real date. From that night on we could not see enough of one another. For weeks we found ourselves messaging one another on Myspace and Facebook. I didn't have a phone, so whenever an opportunity presented itself, I managed to schedule a time to speak to her and find one.

This continued for a few months until we found ourselves at my friend Levi's. We had just had a night of spending time with Levi and his girlfriend at the time. As the night grew closer to an end; Jessica had to leave. Helping her gather her things I decided to walk out to the parking lot with her to walk her to her car. It was a warm summer evening and the wind lightly grazed across the two of us as we walked to her car. Approaching her Jeep, she held her keys in her hand as we both looked nervously at one another. It had been one hell of a month, however, we had never really established what we were.

"So, I feel like we have been kind of dating for a while now, even if we haven't called it that." Trying not to stutter as my cheeks began to blush in a rosy red fashion.

Looking down to her keys as that beautiful smile once again slid across her face "Yea I guess so, we should probably make it official then huh?"

Officiating the exclusiveness to one another I would tell her goodnight and turn to walk away.

"Can I... get a hug..." She giggled.

"Yes!" I laughed awkwardly.

Embracing one another under the evening sky we would finally kiss. As our lips connected, all of my worries and concerns of the world seemed to slip away. I had never felt anything like this before. Despite all of the ridiculous things that had transpired over my years, for the first time I felt content with the world. My world that had been so darkened by the traumas that haunted me; I finally found the color to my black and white world.

# Nomad's Land

Life had been great. The summer, though nearing its end proved to be the best closing anyone could ask for. Jessica and I were nearly inseparable. My family was working on a haunted house called "The Frenzy". It was a fundraiser for my parents' business they were starting up to help the homeless and those in need. We spent the summer piecing the ideas together, however, Halloween was approaching and now it was time to build.

My parents had found an old paper mill that they were able to rent out for the season. It had a fifteen thousand square foot warehouse that we were going to transform into one of the best-haunted attractions for that year. Days on end we devoted hours to creating a massive wooden maze of horrors. A designer was hired to plan the whole thing out. She was the mastermind behind the event. We just helped build it. The empty warehouse quickly evolved from an empty warehouse into a spooky, prop filled establishment. With the age of the building and the eerie echoes that could be heard through-out it, it made a perfect venue. It didn't even feel like we were in the same world by the time we had finished constructing it.

October came and went just as quickly. We devoted weeks to the planning and building of the haunted house.

Finally, we launched it. It was a major success. We were rated one of the top haunted houses in the state. It was a miracle that a year prior we weren't even sure where we would be living, to now raising enough money to help other people in need. It was amazing. Not to mention fun.

During the same time, we spent working on the haunted house, an old face would resurface into our lives. Marge had decided she wanted to return home. Despite the many objections from my father, Gemma had given him an ultimatum.

"Let her move back in, or we are getting a divorce!" She exclaimed, putting her foot down.

My father, though knowing better, could not say no to the love of his life. Standing in defeat, he allowed it.

Marge appeared to be making a real attempt to change her life around. She had given up the chasing of boys and parties it seemed. She had decided she wanted to return to school but didn't have the money.

"Hey David, so I found a CNA class at the tech center. It's seven hundred dollars though. Would you be able to lend me some money to get started?" Marge requested, standing outside our yellow, recently restored house.

"I can see what I can do." I didn't have a lot of money at the time, but I had been working some side jobs to try and stay afloat. I had been attending college for nearly a year now and had saved some of my money from my grants. Thinking it was for a good cause, and for family, I decided to lend her the money.

"Ya I can stop at the ATM I guess before I head down to the haunted house. I'll drop the money to you later." I said nervously.

As we have learned from previous endeavors though, no reward comes without punishment. While we had a successful Halloween season, November is where the horrors would once again resurface. Marge had been back in the home for less than two weeks, and trouble was already stirring inside her maniacal head.

One evening Jessica and I had left the warehouse to return to her mother's house. I had been staying there nearly every night at this point. We had laid in bed for only a few short minutes before I received a phone call that began one of the biggest trials ever.

"Hey, David." My father greeted me with a weary sigh.

"Hey, Dad, what's up? We were just getting ready for bed." I replied, unknowing of what was coming.

"You're never going to believe this. I'm out of the house again. After we put the kids down for bed, Marge went upstairs to Mildred's room. Not even fifteen minutes later she came downstairs just a' yellin and hollerin and hittin me. She said that Mildred said I have been molesting her." He again sighed. The weight could be heard in his voice.

Just as he spoke the words, all of the worries of all of the previous demons of my past resurfaced.

"I'll be right there!" I said with a horrified look on my face.

After hanging up the phone I looked to Jessica,

"We need to go right now!"

"What's going on?" She exclaimed, sitting up quickly in the bed looking just as confused as she was worried.

"Marge is at it again. She said my dad was molesting my little sister. I don't want to go through this shit again!" I stated angrily. Quickly scooping my jacket and keys into my hands.

We rushed out the door and went to the car. Quickly buckling our seat belts we drove off. Paying no attention to speed, my world began to quickly narrow. Knowing well what to expect in the next coming days, I couldn't focus on the day at hand. Hundreds of memories of the foster home rushed through my head. The abuse, the neglect, the counselors. Was our family cursed? Were my younger brother and sister going to face the same traumatic fate I once had? It was too much to process. I rapidly pulled into the driveway not even bothering to shut the car off. Marge stood outside of the house smoking a cigarette. The anger grew heavily inside me as I flung the door open. My mouth began to run faster than the car I drove home that evening. Before I knew it, I was shouting at her. I knew she had concocted the whole thing, just as she had in the past. Still screaming I felt a hand slap across my face and begin pushing me. Just as quickly as I arrived I had found myself just as quickly leaving.

The whole thing was troubling. Who do I believe at this point? Could it have happened? I didn't want to have to pick between my siblings and my father. We had already been broken apart before. Without even a moment to process my attempts at deducing what was true and what wasn't, wondering if there was some scheme to be had out of this; my phone rang once again. This time, however, it wasn't my father. It was another familiar voice. One that I would not have expected to hear from so soon. Especially within less than an hour of the events that had just transpired. It was my mother. Now I knew, something wasn't right.

"Hey, buddy!" My mother would begin, in her same squeaky voice as always.

"Hi, mom." I began with a blunt response.

"I heard what's going on, are you ok?" Again, inquiring empathetically.

"How did you hear about it?" I asked, puzzled at how quickly news like this would make it to her.

"Well, Marge called me." She responded.

Trying to process the relation between the two since neither Marge nor Mildred had any relation to my mother struck me as odd, I hung up the phone and sat silently thinking to myself. Then it all came together. Anytime a malicious scheme would come into play, and the stone of allegations was cast, my mother was always found closely behind the rock.

Our next few months proved to be troubling. Before long both Harry and Mildred were removed from the home. Since I even questioned rational thoughts, I too was removed from the family. I wasn't allowed to see my siblings anymore. I had to attend supervised visits with the two, and even those were short-lived. Soon after they both had been relocated. Except now, I was not allowed to see them at all.

The caseworkers told me all I had to do was say my dad was guilty, and I could see my siblings again. Yet, even though I was torn in wanting to support both my sister and my father, I couldn't bring myself to cave. There was much that seemed all too suspicious to me. It was argued that she had been raped three times a day, every day, for two years straight. It was a horrific thought. Yet, when the medical examiner came back stating they found no abnormalities I began to question even more. Since we had rebuilt the home I had spent random hours of coming and going from the house. Most of the time sleeping on the couch as that had been a comfortable spot for me from my bouncing around the years prior. Not long after, my sister even admitted she had lied, and was told to say those things. Once she said that; anyone that disbelieved her initial claims of abuse was allowed to see her. It was like she was confiscated from the world. Anyone who did not support the initial claims were one by one removed and threatened.

I was thankful to not feel like I was embarking on this unfortunate journey alone this time. As my family and I drifted further apart, it only pulled Jessica and me closer together. February abruptly came. For the past few weeks, Levi and I would covertly sneak away to hang out while he helped me pick out the perfect ring to solidify my growing love for Jessica. Re-entering the stomping grounds of my birthplace of Grand Rapids, we had journeyed to a local jewelry store where I would gawk at dozens of shiny rings I knew I wouldn't be able to afford. After nearly an hour of gazing into the clear glass boxes as the security guard and staff watched the internal struggle taking place inside of me; I had finally found something I knew I could make work. Sitting at the back of the display case were coupled rings. One was a gold and silver band clearly designed for a man; the other was a silver ring with a glistening diamond. It wasn't the most majestic in the store, but it was beautiful. After tossing the idea to Levi, I managed to find my way into accepting the much-pressed credit card offer from the store. I didn't care what it would take, I had to have this. Jessica deserved at least that.

The day was approaching, my plan was set and I was determined to make this happen. Despite the horrific events of the year, Jessica and I deserved our happiness. I had planned a trip to Chicago. I had seen an ad that showed a magnificent display where a tunnel led through the Shed Aquarium. That was it! I wanted to pop the question in that spot. Jessica had never seen the ocean before and hadn't been to the aquarium. I couldn't afford to get her to the ocean, but I would damn well try my hardest to bring her as close as I knew how. February 13th approached rapidly, almost quicker than my heart pounding at the nearing approach. We woke up that morning, she knew of the intended trip, but not of the intended purpose. Michigan was notorious for snowing at the most inopportune time. The roads were horrible. Looking out into the pale, chilled, desert-like frost; nothing was going to stop us today. We began our trip, hand clenched tight to the steering wheel as my eyes squinted to keep on the safe trail of the highway. Nearly ten miles from our home, my curse attempted to cripple my desired plans. My tire went flat. Limping my car along, like the little engine that could, I was able to make it to a local tire shop at the Otsego Belle Tire, just one town over from where we were living. As we pulled the car in and were told the cost and time; Jessica was overwhelmed.

"Screw it, we just weren't meant to go today. It has already been a difficult day, I'm done!" She huffed defeated.

"I'm so sorry babe, we can still do this! We will just be a couple of hours behind. We can still have a fantastic day." I encouragingly pried. I knew what was at stake. I had given in to defeat so many times before in my life. But Jessica deserved more than that defeat. I was not giving up. The clerk rounded the corner to let us know our vehicle was ready. Excited, and eager to return to the marvelous plan I had organized we continued on our trip.

Arriving into the busy city as we passed over the bridge leading into the heart of Chicago; darkness began to cloak the sky. Jessica's anxiety rose as we weaved in and out of traffic attempting to keep up with the busy chaos of such a large city. This was slightly worse than what I was used to in Grand Rapids, however, I was not an amateur at city driving. With a sigh of relief from her and me, we finally reached our destination. As her nerves calmed, mine increased drastically. It was almost time. Entering the large aquarium I subtly patted my pocket to ensure I had the ring. I nervously walked with her up the large stairs as we entered the aquarium. She began to catch on that I had shifted to a more fidgety and giddy school girl. I quickly reached for a map to find the perfect spot I had planned out. I wanted to pop the question as soon as possible. Much to my demise, the spot I had envisioned was not at this location. Frantically I put my detective skills to use. I had to come up with something quick. I was not going to deter from my mission today. Then I saw it. The perfect spot in front of the dolphins.

We waded through the busy crowds as we discovered the exotic creatures we were not acclimated to seeing in our everyday lives. She was glowing with excitement unaware that the best was yet to come. Making our way past the penguins we came to a small cookie stand. Booths sat across from the glass display as the creatures waddled in and out of the water.

"Let's get a cookie." I exclaimed excitedly.

"Ok, I'm not really hungry, but we can split one." She replied with a smile.

As we sat in the booth, my mind was racing. Knowing the next stop was the spot. Just up the stairs behind me would enter into a large opening, in front of a wall of windows with majestic dolphins acrobatically floating out of the water of the tank directly facing out to the gorgeous view of Lake Michigan. Fumbling in my pocket in a manner I had hoped was not noticeable, I retrieved the ring and subtly placed it in my pocket.

"Are you okay?" She inquired with a giggle.

"You seem nervous." She questioned.

"I'm just excited to be here with you." I exclaimed, realizing I was about to give away the big reveal.

"Awww, me too!" She giggled.

I finished the last bite of the cookie I didn't really want but needed to stall for the grand moment. I brushed off the table as we both stood. Taking her by the hand we walked up the wide turning stairwell. The excitement building, my heart pounding, hands sweating, we emerged to my masterfully envisioned spot. However, just as the day had promised, the dolphins were closed. Apparently that day a Beluga Whale was pregnant and ready to give birth any day. They had moved the dolphins to accommodate the pregnant mammal. We entered the open area with the beautiful view of the lake and the boarded off Beluga tank, where my dolphins should have been.

"Fuck it!" I thought to myself. This is happening now.

Gently grasping Jessica's hand I spun her towards me. Not nearly as finessed as I would have liked. Eyes locked with one another as the grand view stood to my left and her right. People passed by unknowingly about to be a part of this magical moment. Dropping to one knee I reached into my pocket and retrieved the beautifully decorated diamond ring. As I extended my hands up I dropped to one knee producing the shiny jewel. Her hand rushed to her mouth. Here it is, the words I have been waiting to hear. The moment this entire day had led up to.

"Jessica, I love you so much. Will you marry me?" I asked nervously as the words somehow managed to fluently slide from my lips.

"Oh no!" She exclaimed as her cheeks lit up with excitement. That same glistening smile erupting across her face just as the first day we met.

"Not quite the words I was hoping to hear." I nervously and jokingly remarked.

"YES! Oh my God, I am just really shy. I don't like making a scene in front of people, but YES." She finished placing the ring on her finger. Standing up we embraced one another as our lips connected to the always much desired passionate kiss as the newly engaged couple. Despite the surroundings of my life, at this moment, I was in heaven.

It had been a taxing year, both emotionally and physically. As much as I wanted to reside in that passionate and remarkable moment, I had to return to the life I so desperately wanted to escape. The court proceedings were going on for nearly a year. Eventually, we were nearing the end of the trial. Gemma, Jessica, my father, and I were walking up to our apartment. Gemma had groceries in her hands as she approached the doorway. She planned a breakfast for all of us. We walked to the doorway leading up the stairs to my and Jessica's apartment that we had moved into just a few months prior. As Gemma reached for the doorknob my father's phone began to ring. While his phone recited its quirky ring tone, we all froze, looking to one another as our hearts sank and our bodies clenched in anxiety. It was his attorney.

"The jury has made a decision. It is time to come back to the courthouse for the decision." She said.

Gemma looked back at my father fearfully. Our hearts all dropped. The world fell silent as the percussive thuds of our heartbeats could be heard, one by one, as the color quickly faded from our faces.

"What does that mean!" Gemma asked, trying to hold back the tears from trickling down her face.

"That came back too quick!" She continued.

My father straightened himself up and buttoned his jacket. Calmly embracing each one of us in a warm hug as he began to offer his words to comfort us.

"It will be okay you guys. Whatever happens, is going to happen. I love you!" He said with a calming smile.

He walked back to his car as Jessica, Gemma, and I walked back to ours. We all arrived at the courthouse where Levi was waiting to show his support. Walking to the glass doors of the courthouse, approaching the tall brick building, we all filed in one by one. The sheriffs had greeted us as they handed us a white bucket to place our belongings in before walking through the two bars that, regardless of how much you empty your pockets, always seemed to emit that loud ringing annoying "buzz". They pulled their wands out systematically scanning each of us as we passed through the doors. Pointing their wands down the hall as each one of us passed the magic wand test, we were given our belongings back and continued on our way. We walked down the hallway towards the room. This had felt like a walk down death row. Not knowing what was waiting for us on the other side. Hand in hand Jessica and I trudged down the ever-narrowing walkway. My father, slightly ahead with his attorney. We opened the two large, heavy, wooden doors and entered the room. All eyes peering at us as we take our seats and my father approached the table with his counsel.

"All rise" the bailiff sternly says.

The judge, in an all-black robe, entered the room and took his seat. We sat in anticipation, unable to take our eyes off of the jury as one stood with paper in hand ready to make the most significant difference in many lives that day. One by one the charges were read aloud before the courtroom. Each ending in what was some of the most heart striking words I would ever hear.

"Guilty." They read

Sequentially, each of the eight counts came back with the same words, equally stripping a piece of my heart away with every word spoken. My body stopped. The world before me stopped. Shaking in my chair, anxious and broken. Tears filled my eyes as I arose, pleading with the officer to be allowed one more hug from my father as they approached to place the steel shackles on both of his wrists.

"You cannot touch the prisoner" they exclaimed.

Words I did not ever envision having to hear spoken. The one who has given so much guidance. My mentor, my protector, my father; hauled away before my eyes. Ready to collapse in the courtroom as they took him away, tightness gripped my chest as if I had just been crushed by bricks, my vision blurred as I fought to catch my breath; slamming the chair behind me, I stormed out of the courtroom doors. Closely behind me, Jessica and Levi hurried to catch up as I left the courthouse. Making it only a few steps before my car, I could no longer hold on to the building emotion, ready to erupt. Like a bottle filled to the brim, emotions poured from my body as the tears flooded the pavement beneath my feet. My world as I knew it has again, crashed down around me in a fiery flame.

Time went by as I attempted to re-adjust to this new life. The brothers and sisters I grew up with all faded away around me. They would tell me;

"If you won't say your dad is guilty, we're done with you!" They would say.

With all of the facts, all of the information, and all of the knowledge; I could not bring myself to sell my soul for blood. In my heart, mind, and body I knew of my father's innocence. If that meant I would now embark alone in this world, absent of family then so be it. I may not have them, but I would still be me.

Papers published with the headlines of my father's conviction. The comments flooded the opinions section where I too was going to be condemned. "The pedophile apple doesn't fall far from the pedophile tree" the opinions section of the local paper read. "They better look into his son" others would exclaim. I was no longer able to show support for my beliefs. I was slandered in the public eye. Truth and logic are no longer applied in this world. It was forever vetted based on the mere emotional weight of the topic. Never had I felt more of a connection to what the "Witches" of Salem must have felt. Regardless of their innocence, the minds were made up.

Weeks continued without my father. Some felt longer than others when I had a bad day or encountered difficulty. Not having the person that always helped guide me weighed heavy on me. Not having the person to help me learn how to grow up. It was hard at times. I had continued my schooling and moved forward with my fiancé. Jessica and I struggled to make ends meet at times, but we always pulled through. I had been working for a short while at a local pizza place while she pulled long evening hours third shift at a gas station. We made just enough every month to cover the cost of rent with a few spare dollars to order groceries.

Another year passed by as Jessica and I faced the elements of the world together. Trying to learn ever quickly how to grow up faster. A few times before I had considered joining the military, but had never really fully committed. I always found some new reason why I shouldn't yet. However, the time came where I could no longer stand the despair of our day to day struggles. Jessica, who stood by me during some of my most lonely times, deserved more than what a minimum wage pizza gig could offer. Fed up with our struggling; Jessica and I laid in bed one evening. Trying to figure out how we were going to make rent and pay bills we both laid there silently. The fan whizzing near the doorway as the moonlight peered through the slightly open shades. I had no family left, but my fiancé and uncle. I looked at her.

"Babe, what would you think if I joined the Army?"

My eyes partially squinting to cloak my hesitancy.

Thinking back to when Chuck had left for the Marine Corps, I too had pondered the concept of enlisting in the military. Looking for stability to care for my soon to be wife, it seemed like the right path for us. I knew it would a burden for us both while I would be away, but it offered opportunities for a better life for us. I had spent so much time dwelling on my family in the past, I needed to secure a positive future for Jessica and myself in hopes for a better life.

Jessica, with a slightly taken aback look, gave a warm calming smile after a moment's pause as she placed her soft hand on my cheek.

"You know whatever you decide to do, I will support you." She replied, giving a soft kiss to my forehead.

The next morning, we both awoke. A card that I had tucked away in my wallet for weeks finally found its way back to my hands. "Staff Sergeant Rogers" it read with a number peering back at me. I placed the card back in my wallet, grabbed my keys, and Jessica and I closed the door behind us as we went out the door to my closest friend Levi's house. We walked in with no time to spare.

"Levi! What would you think about joining the Army with me?" I exclaimed excitedly.

"Sure, let's do it." He said without a moment's hesitation.

Shortly after, he and I jumped back into the car together and took off. In no time we found ourselves at a nearby recruiting station. We both walked in to find a short-haired, camouflage clothed, uniformed, stocky man sitting behind the desk. Motivational posters lined the walls promising things such as "Courage!" "Leadership!"

"Be part of something bigger than yourself!" Being in the presence of men and women who had done amazing things gave a sense of purpose.

"Staff Sergeant Rogers?" We asked.

Standing up behind the desk to greet us, he extended his hand.

"That's me!" He said. "What can I do for you boys?"

We each shook his hand before I reached back to my wallet to grab the card he had given me some time previously.

"I received this card from you some time back. My friend and I are ready to join!" I said as we both looked at one another with slight hesitation, nervousness, and excitement in our voices.

"What are you boys looking to do?" Extending his hand to the two chairs in front of his desk he would pull the base of his jacket down to remove any incriminating creases from his nicely pressed uniform.

"Whatever you have open. We can drive trucks; we can do whatever you need us to!" We naively stated as we pulled back the chairs to take a seat.

"Well, I do have a few slots open for Chemical, Biological, Radiological, Nuclear Specialists. It even comes with an $8000.00 bonus!" He remarked proudly.

Without a moment of delay, Levi and I looked to one another, interested in the fancy title, we looked back to Staff Sergeant Rogers,

"We'll take it!" We exclaimed.

We had no idea what we had just agreed to, but we knew it was exciting.

Preparing for our new journey, Levi and I sat to fill out

paperwork. Page after page we signed a portion of our life away as we granted permission to search into our past. The paper stack began to shrink, becoming thinner, as we completed the daunting task of tedious swoops with the pen. We again shook the hand of Staff Sergeant Rogers as he gave us our report dates to Lansing. This was where we began to make sure we were qualified, and ready to become one of the world's fiercest fighting forces. Within a few short weeks, we found ourselves in a government bus taking us to the Military Entrance Processing Station, for short, MEPS. This was where we could experience our first embarrassing stories of doing duck walks in our underwear and being poked and prodded for verification of our ability to perform in harsh conditions.

After the grueling hours of "hurry up and wait" we finally approached the office with our stack of papers in hand, ready to speak with a counselor to give us the final blessing to sign our lives away. Sitting down, paper by paper, they sift through them. Nodding and mumbling until finally,

"One more signature here" they would say.

Reviewing our contract and confirming our job duties and entrance ranks, I finally placed the pen to the paper, signing the last bit of freedom away to Uncle Sam. I handed the paper back to the counselor as I was escorted to a large room with paneled wooden walls. Flags of each military branch lined the room leading to a small stage with circled emblems placarding the wall behind them. I approached alongside many of the other candidates who as well have just signed their last free document. We approached the stage and were asked to extend our right hand.

"I, David Kranz, do solemnly swear that I will support and defend the Constitution of the United States against all enemies, foreign and domestic; that I will bear true faith and allegiance to the same; and that I will obey the orders of the President of the United States and the orders of the officers appointed over me, according to the regulations and the Uniform Code of Military Justice. So help me God!" Proudly reciting the words presented to me. I lowered my hand as I am again, filled with pride and purpose.

That evening I rushed back home to Jessica, excited to tell her the news, and able to say

"Babe! It's official! I am in the United States Army!"

"Congratulations! I am so happy for you!" She spoke back excitedly.

"The downside, I do ship out in April," I responded with a downturned look.

Jessica looking to me, trying to remain happy,

"That's only three months away?" she said, holding back her tears as worry filled her body.

"I know baby, but I will only be gone for a few months. So many good opportunities can come from this!" I explained, trying to ease the sadness arising from the decision that will separate us for a short while. I was joining as an Army Reservist. This gave me the opportunity to still serve my country and gain a new purpose while being with my lovely soon to be wife while pursuing my academic endeavors.

Having been engaged for nearly three years we knew the best decision would be to wed before my departure. After much discussion, and both agreeing we did not want, or need a fancy wedding, we lined everything up.

We would hold a small ceremony and be married in a church by a family friend who was a pastor.

It was April 2012, only one week remained before my departure. We couldn't have asked for a more glorious day. The sun shined especially bright for us as the spring colors illuminated our surroundings. By the end of this day, we would be married. My soon to be bride emerged from the back of the chapel in a beautiful white dress. The world around us couldn't compete with her beauty that day. The seasons were put to shame with a single breathtaking glance at my wife to be. Her beautiful brown hair extravagantly draped down in waves with the same glistening smile I adored, so pure and white, as she walked down the aisle. As she approached we seized this last moment with one another. The world around us froze, except, this time it was on our terms. We spoke the much-awaited words to express our love and commitment to one another. Moments later, we signed the paper that would verify our marriage.

While the chapel was filled with her family and friends, my families I had acquired over the few short years in Allegan also attended to show their support for me. Levi was my best man accompanied by Travis. Their families sitting in the pews gleaming with smiles honoring happiness they too knew I desired. Though I had missed my father dearly, and it was not the family I had once envisioned being present at a special time like this; I was still surrounded by family.

Later that evening we all gathered back at her mother's house. A small trailer, but large enough for us to enjoy the beginning of our new life with one another. A beautiful homemade cake from Jessica's aunt was brought into the dining area and placed on the table with a wax bride and groom decorating the top of the sweet white-bordered cake. Taking a large knife in my hand, Jessica wrapped her soft hand around mine. We made our first cut into the cake. Each of us grabbed a piece as we offered it to the other. Simultaneously as the pieces neared closer to our mouths; we each thrust the sponge-like cake into one another's faces. We each let out a smile with laughter as the frosting covered our noses and face. We were both happy. The world that had caused so much pain for the two of us, at this moment, stood still. Silent, and allowing us to take in one another's eyes. We seized the moment.

Only two weeks passed. Most couples who had been married would soon be finding themselves on a beautiful ocean, or a beach somewhere embarking on the glorious freedom gaze of nature; hand in hand with margaritas. This was not the case for us, however. My shipping date approached so rapidly. It felt as if we didn't have nearly enough time to enjoy one another before uncle Sam asked that I uphold my end of the bargain. We packed my bags and enjoyed our last evening with one another before I departed for five months to learn how to better protect our country. The following morning came when we packed up the trunk of our Dodge Charger. We drove to Kalamazoo together, hand in hand, not wanting to let go. With my manila packet in hand, we made our way to the airport. Giving one last embracing hug, grasping one another passionately before she would connect her lips with mine and we gazed once more into each other's eyes. Both of ours filling with tears.

"It will be quick," I assured her.

"Not quick enough" She giggled, trying to force down the tears.

"I will write to you every chance I get!" I promise.

"You better!" She said eagerly.

"Now Boarding" a voice bellowed over the intercom of the terminal.

Looking back at my breath-taking wife, tears both filling our eyes once again we say our final goodbyes. Not knowing where this journey would take me, she blows me one last kiss as I make my way onto the plane. Within an hour I found myself from Kalamazoo to O'Hare, hours later from O'Hare to Atlanta. I exited the plane and gathered my belongings where I was directed to wait outside. It was late in the evening when we found ourselves sitting outside the airport. Taking in the last hit of a much-desired cigarette, young men lined up beside me. Finally, a bus arrived in front of us as a uniformed man stepped off. Tall, broad, and fearless; his eyes pierced out at us staring each of us down.

"LINE UP!" He shouted sternly. "From this point forward, any alcohol, tobacco, or drinks will be discarded into the trash before you get on my bus. Do you understand me!" He again roared. "Now, in a single file fashion, line up and place your belongings under the bus. Once you're done, line back up and get on the bus." He finished.

Quickly rushing to comply we did as we were asked before we lined back up and stood fear-stricken waiting for further direction. I'm almost certain the same thought passed through each of our minds; "What the hell did we get ourselves into!" That would be the last free thought that would pass through our minds as we entered the bus and shipped out.

# Easy Company

We rode on the bus for what felt like hours. No lights, no talking, so silent I was sure I could hear everyone's thoughts. We came to a lit up town. As we approached we found ourselves passing through a tall statue with two soldiers facing one another. "Welcome To Fort Benning" the sign read. Though I was nervous, it was a marvel to be seen. I had never been this distant from home. Though I had learned to adapt to new environments, this was the first time I was completely alone. I didn't have friends, I didn't have my father, I didn't have my wife. This was something I could do that was larger than myself. Even though I felt much pride, I as well felt much fear.

My heart began pounding as we came closer and closer. My nerves that were slightly calmed had begun to resurface. The bus came to a halt. All was silent for only a moment as we all watched the doors slowly open to the bus. A brown round hat first emerged, shortly followed by whatever it was underneath it. Not human, I was certain of it!

"Get off my bus now! He shouted.

"HURRY UP! YOU'RE ON MY TIME NOW!" He continued to yell. Each man on the bus scrambling to get into some sort of a line to comply as quickly as possible.

Each of us rushing off of the bus looking around the ground to find our sprawled out bags. Never had I felt so disoriented. We each gathered our belongings after a very distraught, gaggle of a mess flailed in front of the large brick building. We filed in one by one, bag in one hand, paperwork in the other. Benches sat in rows as we entered the building. Pictures of great warriors decorated the walls with flags and emblems of the service branches. Each of us were directed to a seat on one of the benches and instructed to sit. Bag underneath the bench, paperwork in hand, sitting straight up knees equally apart and parallel toes pointing straight ahead on the floor with our hands resting on our laps. One by one each of us were called and directed to a different section where we began our in-processing.

The men that surrounded me, all equally tired, could not help but wonder when we would be readily able to finally get some rest. That, however, I would learn, would be one of the silliest thoughts to pass through my mind for the next ten weeks of my life. Sleep, though desired, was not a gift for a soon to be soldier. You see, when I first joined the military I thought I was able to call myself a soldier. Silly me. I would find that instead, at least for the next ten weeks, my name was private. Or shithead... or whatever clever title came to mind for one of my many drill sergeants.

We began in processing, for a week we marched from one side of the base to the next attempting to learn different tunes and how to form a proper formation walk. It didn't matter how good of a singing voice any of us had. We all sucked. Not only did we all suck, but we would learn to embrace it. Clever huh? We would learn that "embrace the suck" would be a phrase we would frequent daily.

A few days in, as we were all eager to get "downrange" as we called it, a few of my fellow privates decided that it was a good time to rough house in the barracks. Before "downrange" could begin you see, the drill sergeants couldn't "smoke" us as they called. Push-ups, sit-ups, V-ups. All of these posed risk for potential injury before being able to break us down and shape us. Instead, however, as the roughhousing began, one of the kids fell into the brand new barracks wall placing a large, body-sized imprint in the drywall. Drill Sergeant came to see what all of the ruckus was when without a second of hesitation he saw the gaping hole in his barracks.

"WHAT IN THE ACTUAL FUCK PRIVATES!" He screamed, echoing through the many bunks and lockers.

"EVERYONE DOWNSTAIRS, TOE THE LINE, NOW!" He continued as a large vein pulsated down the side of his neck.

Rushing downstairs we all filed in a formation, sloppily, and gaggled.

"TODAY PRIVATES, YOU ARE GOING TO MAKE UP FOR THE DAMAGE TO MY BUILDING!" He began.

"Instead of fixing my wall, you are going to work it off! You see that field over there? It needs to be mowed, and lucky for you we have all afternoon to get that done!" He continued as we all glance at the massive track field in front of us.

"Grab your battle buddy, grab a trash bag, and get to cutting!" He finished.

One kid, foolishly unaware of how to keep quiet

inquired, "Drill Sergeant, where are the supplies?"

Drill sergeant began to smirk as he raised one hand with a slight chuckle. "Each of you has all that need right here!" He replied, holding his arm up coiling his thumb, pinky, and ring finger in as he began clipping his index finger and middle finger together indicating a scissor.

Hours passed as we baked under the Georgia sun. My battle buddy holding the black trash bag as I reached down clipping another batch of grass blades between my fingers. Finally, we heard our much-awaited saving hail us from the patio.

"Alright privates, form it up!" The drill sergeant shouted.

Without the slightest delay, each of us gathered our bags and rushed back to the shaded concrete patio. Forming up we were told to sit. Setting our bags to the side of us as we took our seat, wiping our brows as the salt-filled sweat poured down our faces.

"When I call your name, raise your hand!" He said

Today was the day we were issued our ID Tags and ID. This was it. The day before we could begin day zero. The much-awaited official start to hell. No more burgers, no more sleep. We gathered our belongings after each private collected their belongings and were dismissed back to their barracks. The night felt like it dragged on. We were excited to begin our official training, but equally nervous not knowing what awaited us "downrange".

The next morning, we all lined up in our respective positions on the concrete patio floor. Drill sergeants wandered back and forth down the rows of soon to be soldiers. Each one handing out strings with different colored beads attached to them. The drill sergeant finally made his way to me and handed me a forest green 550 cable with red and black beads lining the short section.

"Tie this on your camelback private." He began.

"Once you have been given your string, gather duffel's and gear and be back down here in five minutes!" He yelled.

Rapidly dashing up the stairs we gather our bags and head back down. This time, even more, drill sergeants lined the walkway.

"Red and black beads, over here!" One drill sergeant yelled.

"Alright privates, listen up! This is your last chance!" He began, "no one will think any less of you, but if you wish to leave this is your chance, after that, you're mine!".

A couple of kids raised their hands as they were escorted to the other side of the busses.

"Alright! That's it! Everyone else, on the bus! MOVE!". They shouted. The echoes could be heard as the stern voices roared through the patios down the road.

We drove for what felt like an hour, feeling like we had just made the same square turns the entire route. That is until we arrived at one building that appeared different. I looked out the window as camouflaged uniformed men with brown round-brimmed hats lined the walkway to a huge brick four-story building. Split into two, it was separated by a sidewalk that led up to a banner reading "EASY COMPANY".

I looked back to the sidewalk trying to take it all in as I saw that as the busses began to come to a halt, the uniformed men began rapidly approaching the busses. This

was called the "Shark Attack". Without any delay, the busses came to a sudden halt. The doors opened as another
brown hat drill sergeant stomped onto the bus, our bags
could be seen from the windows were flung to the ground
outside. There was so much yelling I don't think I knew
what was happening anymore. One second I was taking in
the scene of the building, the next I found myself hauling
ass off the bus rapidly searching for my green duffel bag.
Screaming ensured around us as privates were running
aimlessly in every direction, not nearly close to the satis-
faction of the drill sergeants. Like lions to a gazelle, they
swarmed us one at a time, screaming directions to us as
we attempted to comply, failing miserably.

We found ourselves rapidly dashing to the banner that
read "Easy Company" like we were being herded as wild
animals into a kennel. Approaching a large opening that
rested beneath the two buildings that were connected by
one set of stairs we were filed into quadrants of what we
would learn to know as the CTA.

"THROW YOUR BAGS DOWN NOW!" They shout-
ed as we separated into our appropriate groups. Throwing
the bags into the center of the floor, we all ran back to our
designated groups.

"10 Seconds to find your bags privates!" They yelled.

Counting down we all scurried back towards the bags
we had just thrown down, for some reason, unable to find
what we had just set down.

"TIMES UP! FRONT LEANING REST POSITION!"
They yelled as we all laid supine on the ground with our
elbows forming a 90-degree angle.

"ONE, TWO, THREE, ONE!" They yelled in unison as

we performed push-ups.

We continued this game for nearly an hour, running back and forth from bag pile to bag pile, unable to find our bags. So many push-ups had been performed that none of us could retain the count, let alone comprehend what was going on. Finally, after we continued to fail the requests, we were eventually told to gather our stuff. We again found ourselves led to another holding area where they went through our bags ensuring we had all our necessary items and no contraband. Again, even during the shakedown, we could not comply in the appropriate time given. More push-ups would ensue, this time with sit-ups, v-ups, and any other manner of fitness you could imagine. Yet, no matter how tired you were you couldn't bring yourself to give up.

Finally, we came to the last bit.

"Alright, Privates listen up! Grab your phones, you have 30 seconds to make one phone call. Make it count!" They shouted.

Each of us rushing to comply as they peered through our souls to make sure no one tried to cheat their well-devised plans.

"Privates, here is what you will say. I'm here, I'm safe, I love you, Goodbye!". They instructed.

Without any time to explain we all could be heard, almost as if robots repeating the ritualistic assurances to our loved ones. I anxiously waited for my turn, only thirty seconds didn't seem like nearly enough time to hear my much awaited comforting soft voice of my wife. Grabbing the phone and praying she would answer, I quickly dialed her number. As it rang, I heard the most beautiful voice answer. Remembering the script, I couldn't help but deviate slightly. I had to assure Jessica that I so much desired to have longer than thirty seconds from her. I wanted to know how she was, how she was doing, if she was okay. Giving my scripted response, I couldn't help but tell her I loved her dearly and I must hang up. With only thirty seconds I couldn't express how much she meant to me. My time was up as I recited my off-script speech. Hanging up the phone, we knew now that this was it. We had finally reached hell.

We had made it three days into the retched training. I remember it like it was yesterday. It was probably one of the most pivotal moments of my life as a man. Not having anyone to guide me, adventuring into the world on my own I didn't feel like I had much left to offer the world. I had been working at an auto parts store back home. Maybe that was all I was destined to return to. My father had been in prison for a little over a year now and I still had a year left of college to have anything to say I could walk away with. I had just been married, why put myself through this hell? I was done. I couldn't do it. I kept telling myself I was too weak. I remember walking up to my drill sergeant, my battle buddy, Lamb we called him, stood at my side. Lamb had been paired as my bunky. I slept on the top bunk, and he on the bottom. He was much taller than me, but we quickly bonded as a support for one another.

"Drill Sergeant." I nervously said.

"What private?" He replied.

"I'm done, Drill Sergeant. This isn't for me. I can't do this." I shamefully said as the words slipped out of my mouth.

My Drill Sergeant staring at me for only a brief moment, quickly turning to a look of disgust. "Stand fast private-" he spoke while turning the other direction.

Moments passed as he, our First Sergeant, our Captain, and another Drill Sergeant approached.

"What the fuck do you want private?" The First Sergeant requested sternly.

"First Sergeant, I'm done. I can't do this." I again muttered.

"Bullshit Private, get the fuck back in formation" he emitted.

My battle buddy and I turned to look at one another, he smiled at me as we both trotted back into the formation. Moments later one of our senior Drill Sergeants approached me.

"Kranz." He said.

"Yes, Drill Sergeant," I replied.

"What the fuck Kranz, what is this I hear you wanting to quit?" He pressed.

"Drill Sergeant, I hate to be a quitter, but I don't have what it takes." Again asserting my delusional image of self-worth.

"Kranz, what did you do before this?" He asked.

Speaking with him about my father and my automotive sales job back home he let out a brief sigh. Shedding light to a side I hadn't seen regarding any decency since I had arrived on the sand-pits of Georgia.

"Kranz, I get it, we all have a rough back story" He began, "but this is where you assert that difference. Do you want to go back home knowing you quit something I am fully confident you would be able to do? You'll be kicking your ass by morning." He finished.

After discussing with him, I decided to press through. I didn't quite know what it was about his tone, I don't know if it was brushing aside internal cowardice I had hid deep down, but from that point forward I felt invigorated. Not only did I not want to let down my dad, my wife, or myself. But, now I couldn't let my Drill Sergeant down. It may have been a ploy; it may have been just a standard speech he had given a thousand other soldiers before me. However, at that time and at that moment, that was exactly what I needed. Someone to say that I mattered. I had what it took. As a young man figuring out how to navigate through life, that little push added more value than words could describe. Someone cared about my success.

For the next month, I found I could shut my mind off. I could push through the pain, and I could give this my all. I had food, I had shelter, I had friends. I could push through this. Soon sleep became obsolete. We learned to function on anything. Eventually, we found humor even when it would cost us push-ups. I remember one morning after we had finished our physical fitness training at 0500 we were walking back to our barracks to change and get ready for chow. Approaching the CTA one of the privates in the back who was in charge of traffic guard, wearing a road vest and carrying a flashlight had held the entire company up that morning. As we approached the CTA we could hear from the back of our marching formation.

"Private! What the fuck are you doing to that rock?!" One of the Drill Sergeants said.

Our curious minds couldn't resist, fully aware of what it would cost us. We turn to see the private poking the rock with his flashlight as we walked by.

"Nothing Drill Sergeant!" He stood straight and firmly as his cheeks turned red.

"Private, you have desecrated that rock! I don't think it appreciates what you have done to it!" He begins, "Private, I think you owe that rock an apology!" He says rhetorically.

The private standing briefly with a slight confusion on his face turns to face the rock once again. "I'm sorry rock." He says.

"I don't think that was very meaningful-" the Drill Sergeant said.

Meanwhile, we can no longer retain the laughter building in our bellies as we stand in the formation. Simultaneously we all burst into laughter as the Private continued, louder and louder, to gain the acceptance of the rock.

"I'M SORRY ROCK!" he bellowed even louder. All of us attempting to refrain from collapsing in laughter. Even one of the Senior Drill Sergeants found it hard to contain himself.

As the Senior Drill Sergeant let out a burly laugh he turned to us, no longer hiding his smile from the amusement, he orders us to attention.

"Half Right-FACE!" He exclaims. Each of us knew full well that we were about to embark on another fitness journey. It had been weeks of training though, the push-ups were well worth the humor of the moment, however. As we dropped to the front leaning rest position, we began counting off as we pressed the earth below our arms. With the shouts of apology, a faint echo behind us, it was just enough laughter to give us the ability to continue the push-ups.

Months had passed as we all had pressed through the many obstacles Uncle Sam set before us. Many trying and difficult times, but also intertwined with many great memories such as the rock. Nearly ten weeks had now passed as we set out on our final training. This was the big one that would grant us the pin, as well as the title of a United States Soldier. Before we knew it, July 3rd approached. We took the field on the beautiful grass in our firmly pressed and pearly white dress shirts and navy blue pants. Our ribbons and badges decorating our chest displaying our verification that we were now soldiers. Badges displaying each soldier's precision with the M16A4 rifles we had grown to be accustom to carrying every waking moment of the last three months. Some displaying the badges of accuracy with a hand grenade. Our shoes were shined to a point where we could nearly blind an onlooker from the reflection.

That day was much awaited as we proudly lined up. Families filled the stands with well-rehearsed displays being presented on the field just before our graduation. Historical plays were acted out on the field showing the progression and honor of our United States Army. Then we were finally announced. Marching across the field as one fierce company. Easy Company, 2nd Battalion, 47th Infantry Regiment. We would proudly walk as one force across the field, as the words were spoken before our families, before my wife who drove hundreds of miles to see this proud moment. To witness the success and completion of our trying last three months.

I am forever grateful for the days spent there, no matter how hard. As a young man trying to find his way in the world, this was another succession of building me into the man I am today. Nothing would beat me down again. I was able to stand in that field showing not just the families in the stands, not just the many soldiers far better than we newly graduated Privates, but I was able to show myself I was something greater than where I came from. My past didn't define me. Despite my upbringing and trials, this is what helped establish me in the direction that I could call my own. I was re-writing my history and changing the Kranz family curse. I was in charge of my life, and no obstacle would stand in my way ever again.

I went on from this experience to finish my Advanced Individual Training. Shipping out to Fort Leonard Wood. I arrived on July 4th. It was the most beautiful and patriotic celebration I ever witnessed. With only three months to go, I could not wait to return home as a soldier and ready to be in the arms of my beautiful wife.

The graduation from AIT had finished. Jessica was not able to attend, unfortunately. However, I was okay with it knowing we were one day away from our reunion with one another. We left there not only soldiers, but we were now trained professionals in our assigned job. I returned home a Chemical, Biological, Radiological, Nuclear Specialist. We shook hands with one another as the crowds began to dissipate. Each of us sharing our last few stories of the good times we had together through hell and back. Some who attended the full six months with me through basic training to now, and some new acquaintances from the recently completed stint.

We said our goodbyes to one another as we each loaded the busses that would take us home. I arrived at the airport where a few of the new friends had met up to wait for their flight to direct them back to their families. Two of us found the nearest bar. We sat down and ordered our double bacon cheeseburger. The greasy blessing went down nicely with our first cold beer in months. Taking in all of the wonderful aromas of freedom we finished our meal just before boarding our plane back to Kalamazoo. This particular soldier and I had lived just fifteen miles from where my wife and I lived. We both became friends in our advanced training and were blessed in taking the journey together through training, and the return home with one another. We could not wait to be back to our loved ones and familiar friends.

We arrived in the late, cool, September evening. Walking through the terminal with broader shoulders than when we left home just six months prior. Dressed in our camouflage uniform with our clean shaved faces and fresh buzzed haircut we walked down the terminal approaching the luggage area. Even in the late evening, we walked through the two glass sliding doors with many awaiting our return. However, there was only one face I would be able to see. I had been anticipating this return for months. Having carried her picture in my chest from day one. It shared all of the blood, sweat, tears, and dirt from Georgia to Missouri with me. Never leaving my side. Yet, now I could retire that picture. As we parted through the doors my eyes would lock to the most beautifully precious site, my wife. Just as I had been encapsulated so many years prior when we first met, once again I was flooded with that same warming beautiful smile from my wife, Jessica. She leaped to my arms as we lovingly embraced one another, our lips connecting after a long-awaited embrace. Our separation had come to an end. I was home.

# That Kid

Having returned home and settled in I would be given my assigned unit location just an hour north of where I lived. Having come from many adventures in previous months, we would be blessed with a new journey as husband and wife. Less than a year after our reunion, we were faced with one of my largest fears; becoming a father. Jessica told me that we were going to be parents. It was not that I didn't want to have a child. I always wanted to be a father. I especially wanted to be a good father. Knowing the past I had, the scars that lined my heart and body, I was scared of what the world had planned for my firstborn son. We were so happy, yet I was equally afraid. As the day came near we went in for our regular check-up. Going in expecting yet another routine visit, we were told we were not going home. Our boy was ready to come out. We were moved over to the birthing center and taken upstairs where we spent the next few nights. Jessica was situated in the hospital room and given a gown to change into. Not knowing how long it would be I rushed home to gather belongings to prepare for our stay. Hours went by with no change. Hooked up to the many cables monitoring her heart rate, oxygen levels, blood pressure, and contractions. They were looking for any indications this child was ready to jump out. Boy was he stubborn though. We went into the evening again with no change. They gave her medications to help the contractions along. What started as mild cramps soon grew into roaring groans. The pain became unbearable with no change to dilation. Eventually, she decided it was time for the epidural. Sitting on the edge of the bed, crying in pain the man entered the room with a metal tray. Poking and prodding as she gripped a pillow in agony. It was no use. They could not get the epidural to work. Feeling defeated the pain grew even stronger if that was even possible.

Jessica screamed in agony, sweating profusely, grasping the rails on either side of the hospital bed. Bright lights to the back of the nurses shine down towards Jessica, glimmering off of the stainless steel trays surrounding the bed with various gowns and utensils. Breathing deeply as the nurses surround her, attempting to soothe and support, "You're doing great!" The nurse said. I stood to the side, holding Jessica's hand to try to render comfort. "You're doing great babe, just breathe," I say. Cries could be heard as the pains continued to grow. "AAAAGGGGG" she screams. The nurse checks to verify her progress. She had not moved past a three. The pain became too much, she conceded to a cesarean section. The many hours of pain with no progress. I felt terrible, not being able to help her. The nurses left for only a few moments, returning with some papers. "You will need to fill out some papers before we can perform the C-section and inform you of the risks," she says. Jessica gripping the pen like a stress ball, brushing off the words as they spilled from the nurse's mouth, nods in compliance one breath after another.

"That's all, we will be moving you shortly," the nurse says.

As the nurse left the room, an orderly returned explaining they would be bringing me down shortly. They handed me a gown and a cap and told me to just sit here and someone would come to get me when they are ready. It felt like ages. Her bed was released as they wheeled her out of the room and down the hall. This was it. This was a big moment. In less than a few hours, our lives would be changed forever. Standing in the room, right where they left me, I peered out the window anxiously waiting for someone, anyone to come to get me. Every time I would hear steps tapping down the echoing hall I would look back. Several rounds of this transpired before the nurse reemerged to lead me to the room.

"Follow me, Mr. Kranz, we're almost ready for you" she smiled.

I walked anxiously behind her. Taps echoing again through the halls. Every prayer I ever knew passed through my mind. Every possible outcome rushed through my head. The dangerous game of the "what ifs" preyed on my every thought. The anxiety just kept growing. We entered an old elevator in the old ward of the hospital. Slowly it creaked as we descended deeper down the elevator shaft. Finally, it stopped. The doors opened and I was brought into a dark room. I could vaguely see a light-emitting down the hall.

"I'll be right back for you, Mr. Kranz, go ahead and put your gown and cap on now." She again remarked.

Shaking with so many mixed emotions I sat in the empty dark room fumbling to put the blue cloth gown on.

Minutes later she returned "You can go in now Mr. Kranz" She again smiled. I walked down the long dark hallway. A bright light shining out at me as we approached the doorway. In the center of the room, there were several men and women in blue gowns, glasses, and gloves. A bright light shined down on my wife who laid there with her stomach so visibly cut open as they jerked her back and forth with the cuts and moving her body like a toy. I was brought to the head of the table where my wife laid. Awake at that. I couldn't understand how she could be so calm as she was being gutted on a surgical table. It was...rather eerie. She looked at me and smiled.

"Hi baby," she said to me. I brushed my hand through her hair.

"Hi beautiful, how are you feeling?" I ask with a puzzled look, wondering how she could not feel any of what was going on to the other side of the sheet draped in front of her.

"I can't feel a thing!" She said again, smiling.

"Alright Mr. Kranz, we're about ready, would you like to cut the cord?" The doctor asked.

Excited and scared with my nerves pouring with adrenaline. "Ye...Yes!" I said.

"Alright, come right over here" The nurse guided me.

"Just grab right here, yup, just like that. And cut right between the two clips. There you go, good job!" The doctor instructed.

Within only a few short moments the most remarkable feeling would encapsulate Jessica and me. All of the fear, anxiety, nerves, all went away with the most beautiful sound. The sound of our baby boy letting out his welcoming cry. He was here. Our firstborn. Christian Kranz.

Quickly the nurses moved him to the head of the table, the cries echoing for only moments as he was brought to the table where they cleaned him off and wrapped him in a little blanket and a hat. He was rested just to the side of Jessica where their eyes first met. Just like a fairy tale they connected. Within moments they advised they had to move him just briefly as they stitched Jessica back up. This allowed me to finally hold what we have been so nervous about for the past nine months. He rested so comfortably in my arms. I couldn't explain how I felt. Even to this day. The joy, the love, the excitement. It was overwhelming. Everything I had been through, every trial, every hard time. Perhaps it was leading us to this. To have the opportunity to create a life, and give him a better life than we had ever been afforded. That alone afforded us the biggest blessing we could receive.

The years went on as we adapted to our new life with our baby boy. Learning of the other struggles, like trying to sleep. Or trying not to sleep. We juggled school, work, and family. It was a new element that took much adjusting. I soon finished my degree at the local community college. I had reached a step not many in my family had made it to. For the next two years, I pushed through more and more academia. Hovering over books and spending tireless nights writing essays and research designs. Learning of the great philosophers and ancient kings. Well minded geniuses who had explored and discovered much of the human mind. All to hopefully become a great mind of my own. My final semester finally arrived. All of the hard work had paid off. I had graduated as the first in my family to obtain a Bachelor's degree. It was fulfilling.

A few months had passed when an old acquaintance reached out to me. My phone had rung, looking at the number puzzled I would answer it.

"Hello?" I inquired.

"Hi, is this David?" A soft woman's voice asked.

"Yes, it is." Still slightly puzzled trying to place where I knew this voice from.

"Hi, oh my god, I'm so glad I got a hold of you!" She began "It's Laura!"

Laura was my English teacher in high school. She was additionally one of my largest inspirations to accomplish my goals. Over the years she had moved her way up as the principal of our high school.

"So, I don't know if you would be interested or not, but we are getting ready to have our commencement ceremony for the graduates for this year's class. We were hoping you may be interested in being one of our guest speakers as an accomplished alumnus?" She finished.

Slightly taken aback and equally humbled "I would be honored to do that!" I exclaimed excitedly.

She had given me the details and the date. Now I just had to prepare. I've never addressed such a large crowd before. For the next few weeks, I would spend countless hours hunched over my keyboard. Typing, then deleting, typing, and deleting. It felt like a never-ending cycle. That was until it clicked. I knew what I had to write.

The day arrived where I entered the large auditorium, greeted by old teachers and acquaintances. Dressed in my suit and tie I took to the stage where I sat next to the graduating students. Hopefully, ones that would continue to make great changes to the world as the next great minds. My time arrived as my name was introduced and requested to the podium. I slowly approached the podium stand as the bright lights shined down on me. Hundreds of family members and staff filled the auditorium seats. Embracing the moment at hand I reflected back on my once self viewed failure of letting down the alternative system many years ago standing before a podium. I remembered the feeling of defeat after giving the speech in Lansing and having not won. As I reflect back on that day I realized, I hadn't lost at all. I just took a different path to success. Being in front of a stand, once again as an older, wiser man; I recognized I had put our school on the map. I had lived out all of the expectations I had placed on myself many years prior. I was honored and proud of what the alternative school had done for me.

As I took a deep breath, I looked out to see my wife had entered through the back of the auditorium. She had to work on the ambulance that day, so it was not expected that she would make it. However, she did manage, which gave me a great deal of comfort. Letting out a big sigh of relief I began.

"My name is David Kranz. I cannot thank the staff of this school enough for what they have done for me, and many students like me. As students who have never quite fit into the traditional school systems, many of us have come from broken homes. It is the staff such as these that have allowed many of us to find a home away from home. I remember entering the alternative school when I was thirteen years old. I started in the seventh grade in Grand Rapids.

From there I began to understand how the world viewed kids such as ourselves. We were "those kids" or "that kid". There had always been a stigma for students like us that had been out-casted from the traditional system. Most thought of us as druggies, dropouts, dumb, or trouble makers. However, seldom did anyone ask what we were capable of. What could we offer to the world? What are our stories and how did we get here, and what could be done to get us to where we wanted to be? For a long time, I hated the term "that kid" or one of "those kids". Yet, as time went on, I began to use that as fuel for motivation to become something greater. It would burn inside of me building pressure until I was ready to erupt with change. From the time I graduated high school, "that kid" would go on to get an Associate's degree. "That kid" would go on to serve in the United States Army Reserve. "That kid" would return home and begin a family while working two jobs, serving his country, and earning a Bachelors' degree. "That kid" would go on to become a firefighter and emergency medical technician that would hold the hands and help those in need in the most terrifying moments of their lives. "That kid" would go on and save those who had been in cardiac arrest, some giving families a chance to say their goodbye's, and others giving a chance and hope to new beginnings after surviving. I began to take pride in being "that kid". Because that kid would be a survivor. They would face adversity and overcome it, overcome every obstacle that had been presented, look it in the face, and say I am not afraid.

Not knowing where to fit in after my experiences in life from kidnapping, constant battles in and out of the court system, foster care, house fires, and more, these amazing teachers accepted me, and those like me. I remember one of my teachers showing up at my house, just moments after the house had been extinguished. Smoke and ash still surrounded the ground while the fire crews walked in and out of the decimated structure. It was a true testament to the genuine care they provided us.

So standing here before you today I want to first congratulate each and every one of you for facing that adversity and doing great things. Next, I would encourage each of you to embrace being "that kid", take pride in it, and use it as motivating fuel to remind you every day of what you are capable of. Thank you."

As I finished my speech there was a slight pause as I let out a sigh of relief. Looking to the crowd, not a moment later, applause would erupt throughout the auditorium. It was one of the most humbling experiences I had felt. It was a feeling that encompassed that resilience. Not knowing as well until I spoke the words aloud that I truly had changed the course of my life, and it was through this I could look back at the many people, mentors, in my life that were there to influence and guide me to that succession. I would like to say that my past would be the end of my hardships, however, as we all know, life has its agenda. Yet, even having encountered terrible times since my childhood, each of those experiences gave me strength and insight that has allowed me to further navigate through trying times. And for that, I am thankful. When you stand face to face with the gates of hell, not much is capable of shaking you anymore.

Though I have faced trials since I will surely encounter

many more before I close my eyes for their last time. Perhaps those are for another time. This, however, was the story of my crucible. My journey through hell in the darkest times in the darkest moments. How I could find happiness through the chaos and cling on to hope when all felt hopeless. How a boy was forged into a man through the gruesome hardships life tries to throw at each of us.

Though there is much to still experience in this life and new trials to arise to overcome; I had found new truths that guided me out of the dark places I had once found myself in. It was my desire for love that became my enemy. It was my lust for acceptance that outcast me. When I finally released myself from the constraints of what I wanted to be; what I expected to be my fate, I finally became who I was meant to be.

There was much motivation that would stem from my life events. The trials that I thought had crippled me for so long. However, they still sit in my mind to this day; motivating me to remind myself that there is nothing wrong with being different sometimes. I'm not the most agile. I'm not the fittest man in the world. I'm not the smartest or wisest person, yet I am content in my mind and at peace with my direction. The greatest thing was overcoming the fears of the stereotypes of coming from a broken home. Not accepting defeat at every burden. Rather, embracing the hardship to aspire for something better.

I have always believed there are two types of people in this world when bad days try to consume us. Some use it as a crutch or a cry for pity. The problem with that mindset, however, is that there is never any room for growth. Due to the tainted perception created in one's mind, it plagues it with victimization and entitlement. They can never see far enough ahead to accomplish their dreams. Then, some embrace it. We realize the trials that we have been thrown into. Wherever that war may be, inside or out of our mind; we overcome it. Keeping our eyes forward and strive for that resilience. I decided I would not let the world stray me from becoming the things I wanted to be. I can and will embrace it to accomplish the changes I want to see in the world. Changing whatever I can for the better. I trusted that God would work through me to make me into the most complete warrior to face whatever trials of hell on earth. I was cast into the crucible to rise out greater than my former self. In those situations, you may fear, however, it is important to not let that fear consume you, to rule you. You can be resilient and you can be strong. You can know that if you must walk through hell, there is a purpose. And when you come to face those paths it is up to you to decide which direction you will take.

I am David Kranz. And this was my story.

# A Burden Lifted

B efore I dive into the conclusion of this story; I want to thank each and every one of you that has embarked on this roller coaster journey with me. It is truly an honor, and hopefully, an inspiration to anyone trying to navigate a difficult path in their life. We all at some point in our lives will find our own burdens. Resilience is being able to face adversity and come out stronger. You have that ability.

It has been an emotional journey writing this story. It has given me a lot of deep insight into who I am as a person. Who I was as a child, and who I am capable of becoming. Long since the trials of my life, I still work even to this day processing the many instances discussed through out this book. Each one of these has impacted who I am as a person, a father, a husband, and a friend. It is my responsibility to recognize that at times I will fail. I will fall down or fall short. However, it is also my responsibility to pick myself back up.

I know many questions have probably been posed throughout this story. Is my father guilty? Have I reconciled with my many siblings or family? What is my relationship like with my mother now? What is life like now for me? I will begin with probably the most pressing question. Is my father truly guilty, and how do I feel about the numerous accusations throughout my lifetime. I wish I had an easier answer to this question. To be fair, the only people who will ever know the true events are between my father, my sisters, and God. I can only make my opinion based on the events and "evidence" that was provided to me.

As a young man I was gifted by the counselor I spoke down upon earlier in this story. On my eighteenth birthday, I was given a box. In that box contained all of the court transcripts from my childhood to the last trial before my father was convicted. I obsessed over wanting to know the truth. I sat and read through hundreds of papers. Meticulously evaluating each and every page. Searching for an "aha!" moment. Each page I read, and the further down the rabbit hole of my past I went, the more I realized my father had never lied to me. Many of the facts of this story have been recreated through the documents I still possess to this day. Regardless, I know many want to know the hard truth. The fact of the matter is, even with compounding documents, the truth rests with those four people and God.

It has been over a decade since I have attempted to reconcile with many of my siblings. I still think about them frequently and wonder what the young innocent minds I grew up with have evolved into today. Am I an uncle? What would life be like had I tried to reconnect? What would life be like had I taken a different path? The comfort I take is knowing I came from a toxic environment. Opening those doors will answer none of those questions.

In the midst of the immediate journey of my upbringing, my mother and her new husband had two children together. Twins, one boy, and one girl. I grew to love and adore them. At a very young age for them, I wanted to be the big brother they may need some day. Knowing the path my mother was on, if they ever needed, I wanted them to have an escape if it should ever come to pass. I still talk to them to this day. Though I have not had the relationship with them I had desired; I, unfortunately, had removed myself from my mother. Nearly ten years ago, in fear of what could happen to my family if my mother ever wanted to intervene, I cut the final cord for connection with her. I swore to always protect my family and shield them from that version of my life. I wanted better for them, and I did not feel I could safely do that with my siblings. Because of that, I have not tried to reconcile.

Isabelle and I unfortunately have never regained the relationship we once had. I always knew that if ever an opportunity arose, I would love to have what we once did in our bond. I still hear about her well-being and am proud of who she has become. Though, we have not spoken in over a decade. I always wish the best for her as she is in my thoughts daily. The amount of trauma we had endured as children would take a toll on anyone, and that is a bond I will never forget.

My mother and I recently reconnected. We speak monthly now as we try to rebuild the many years of distrust. I have been sure to keep it as much at a distance as I could to ensure the safety of myself and my children. Though it may be painful, I have sent her pictures of her grandchildren, but will never allow them to meet her.

As for me; I continued to reach for the stars. Since my journey in the fire service, I continued my education. With plans to go on to be a psychologist, life as it would have had other plans for me. I began my first year of graduate school when the passionate love I had for the fire service consumed me. In 2018, I was offered the first-ever full-time firefighter position at my department. Knowing the steep journey of graduate work and full-time in a fast-paced high-stress job; I conceded and decided to fully dive into the fire service. It had a calling I could not ignore. I went on to obtain certifications to allow me to help teach new recruits the skills of the trade, most importantly including access to behavioral health. In 2018 with the help of our Fire Chief and City, we integrated the first-ever employee assistance program to help fill the emotional needs in the industry. Though I am not in psychology, I still very much treasure helping people in need. I still love to learn and study philosophy and the human mind, however, the rewards of helping others in the world of public service is my passion.

After the conclusion of this story; Jessica and I went on to have two more children. A beautiful girl and another handsome son. My children have become my world. Though I at times feel I am not doing enough for them, I consistently strive to ensure they have a better life. I still write poetry to this day and dipped my toes into the world of publishing my first book. Never finding a dull moment I learned the human mind is capable of anything with enough drive.

# About the Author

DAVID KRANZ is a Fire Captain and Emergency Medical Technician with the Otsego Fire Department & Rescue. Since he was a child he has dedicated his life to understanding human behavior and helping those in need. While serving in the fire service he became a primary advocate for behavioral health in and out of the service. As an alumnus of Grand Valley State University, his passion is to share his personal stories to bring hope and awareness to adolescents as well as young adults who have experienced trauma and hardship in their lifetime. In this effort he hopes to direct them to a place of peace.

With his background in psychology and philosophy, he uses his own personal examples of the rigorous struggles he has weathered to promote resilience, giving strength back to those who need help finding the light in a darkened world; empowering them to share their stories to guide them to healing.

David still resides in Michigan and continues to serve the members of his community with pride.

CPSIA information can be obtained
at www.ICGtesting.com
Printed in the USA
BVHW080009150521
607267BV00005B/619

9 780578 871516